Why is Contantine a **pocket GIANT**?

Because he was the first Roman Emperor to convert to Christianity.

Because he formally ended religious persecutions.

Because he united the Roman Empire and saved it from collapse.

Because he ignited the flourishing of Christian art and architecture.

DR WERNER DE SAEGER is a professor in the Faculty of Law at the University of Brussels (ULB) and researcher and tutor at the Universities of Oxford and Cambridge. Educated at Harvard, Oxford, Cambridge, Leiden, Brussels, Leuven and Jerusalem, he specialises in the religions, art and architecture, and law of both Classical and Late Antiquity and the modern world.

T0353147

CONSTANTINE

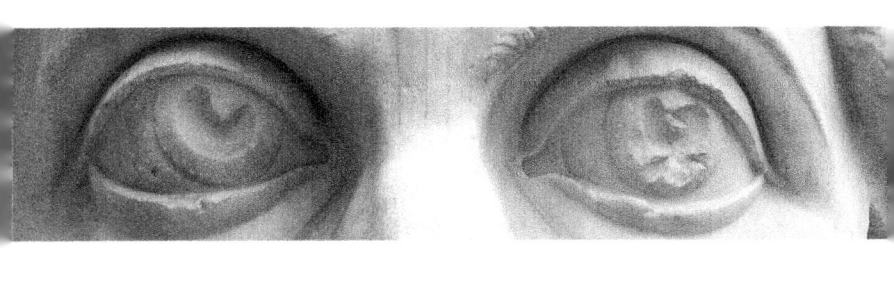

POCKET
GIANTS

WERNER
DE SAEGER

To The Reverend Guillaume Baerts †
sapientia per colloquia

Cover image: © Shutterstock

First published 2016

The History Press
The Mill, Brimscombe Port
Stroud, Gloucestershire, GL5 2QG
www.thehistorypress.co.uk

British Library Cataloguing in Publication Data.
A catalogue record for this book is available from the British Library.

ISBN 978 0 7509 6269 8

Typesetting and origination by The History Press
Printed and bound in Great Britain

Contents

1

Why Constantine is a Giant

Constantine the Great, Roman emperor from AD 306 until his death in AD 337, left a lasting legacy on the Western world. The revolutionary changes in the way the empire dealt with Christianity under his reign were the foundation for the creation of innovative legislation, new types of art and architecture, and hereto unseen theological paradigms. Constantine inherited the leadership of one of four parts of the empire in AD 306 in York, after the death of his father Constantius. At the time the empire was politically structured to be led by four individuals, a system known as the tetrarchy, which was introduced by Emperor Diocletian at the end of the third century. Diocletian had sought to respond to the lack of stable leadership during the imperial crisis of the third century. Although Constantine's role from AD 306 onwards was well defined and geographically limited, over the course of the next two decades he would ruthlessly eliminate the very notion of the tetrarchy and become sole emperor of the Roman world.

During his quest for power over the Roman Empire he turned to Christianity. Whether that choice was well reflected, and inspired by sincere notions of a spiritual conversion to Christianity, will likely remain a topic of eternal debate, as it touches upon psychological analysis and it is near impossible to tell whether a man living seventeen centuries ago was genuine in his theological convictions. Indeed, it is often proclaimed that Constantine used Christianity, and monotheism, in a political strategy to reunite the empire: one emperor, one God. It fits a *post facto* analysis nicely but remains just a theory. It seems more than probable that the emperor was, at least at some moments and up to a certain point, devout in his Christian worldview. His decisions, starting with the very notion of joining a regularly persecuted and small minority on the fringes of Roman society, were too radical and too enthusiastic to have originated out of a purely strategic and/or Machiavellian political philosophy.

As soon as February AD 313, and only a few months after the Battle of the Milvian Bridge on the River Tiber, where he fought Maxentius, and where he supposedly turned to Christianity after having seen a cross in the sky, Constantine declared the persecutions of the Christians to be over. His Edict of Milan could, in a limited sense, be seen as an early type of freedom of religion for all *avant la lettre*. Although he clearly used language and notions foreign to international standards of human rights in the twenty-first century, specifically singling out Christians as one group granted the right to enjoy religious freedom, the edict remains a pivotal point in the history of the politics, laws and religions of the Western world. The very fact that Christians could now openly live their faith triggered changes that would ultimately lead to the supremacy of Christendom at the end of the fourth century, while less than a century earlier they had still been hunted and persecuted. That move, from a modest church discretely meeting for prayer gatherings and communal meals in private houses, to an institutionalised church with not just imperial patronage, magnificent buildings, comfortable finances and a growing demographic reach, but with secular power and influence, is the nexus of the revolutionary shift Constantine ignited.

The humanistic notion of religious freedom dating back to the Edict of Milan in AD 313 was, however, and perhaps unfortunately, not to last very long, as the coercive nature of the secular use of religious power would soon rise. In AD 318, Constantine allocated dispute settlement privileges to bishops, thereby making *de facto* judges out of clergy members. Was this to be seen as a form of *privilegium fori*, the concept of being judged by one's peers? I think not. In this case, we are not merely looking at legal proceedings in which clergy members are involved; any Christian could opt for a case to be heard by a bishop. And during a certain period, the decisions of a bishop seated as judge would be final. The fact that Constantine singled out Christianity for such a conferral of secular power is not to be underestimated. Mixing religion and law was not revolutionary, the formalistic aspects of both Roman Law and certain elements of Christianity, and especially

Paganism, were quite identical, but the consequences were real: suddenly Christians were taking part in the legal, and even politico-legal aspects of government administration.

In AD 321, Constantine established a law that would be known as the Sunday Rest Law. This notion of a weekly day of rest, similar in its philosophy to the Jewish Sabbath, is still applied in many European countries, and in the United States of America, where it is known as 'blue laws'. For one day each week, shops are either closed or not allowed to sell certain products and businesses temporarily shut down operations. The idea of resting from work every seventh day is not new; Judaism had known it for a long time albeit on a different day of the week. Whereas Jewish people to this day celebrate Sabbath from sundown on Friday evening to sundown on Saturday evening, Constantine's day of rest would be the Sunday. This change of calendar was not insignificant; it furthered the parting of the ways, the complex and long process that gradually separated Christianity from its Jewish origins. A change in the weekly day of rest may seem like a minor element if analysed on its own, but it is to be seen as part of an ensemble of changes and distinctions which would culminate in the establishment of an entirely separate Christian identity. Such an identity would align Christians into one community, and try to create a level of orthodoxy at which one could reasonably speak of the Christian Church as one entity, instead of a kaleidoscope of groups and communities which might share common practices but still had a diversity and pluralism that caused strife and enmity. Christians being close to, but still quite different from, one another was indeed one of the challenges Constantine faced when he wished to unite the Church just as he was succeeding in uniting the Romans in one empire. Concurrently though, this Sunday was also the day of rest in honour of the sun god, Sol Invictus. This ambiguity, simultaneously Christian and pagan observation, is what keeps the controversy alive, and deters scholars from forming a consensus on the nature of Constantine's conversion, reign and life.

To reach his objective of unity, and thus to eliminate internal tensions and excessive diversity within the Christian framework of the fourth century is what led the emperor to invite all bishops to an important meeting in Nicaea (modern-day İznik in Turkey): the Council of Nicaea. In AD 325, as various controversies fuelled enmity between the different Christian communities, not least Arianism (an intricate theological debate on the nature of the Trinity, studied to this day in patristics courses), Constantine invited 1,800 bishops, accompanied by priests, deacons and acolytes. Although not everyone participated, and the numbers vary, we know that the meeting was well attended and taken seriously. It was the very first time such an ecumenical council was planned, and its single objective was to reach doctrinal unanimity on a variety of topics. Agreement was reached on the Trinity, thereby condemning Arianism, and furthermore on the date of the celebration of Easter, as well as a series of internal issues on Church discipline. Twenty canons (hence canon law) were announced, and a creed (the declaration and summary of the Christian faith), known as the Nicene Creed, was created.

It is not only his politico-legal changes that make Constantine a giant. The abstract notions of law and political leadership resulting from the emperor's turn to Christianity may well be crucial and do indeed trigger societal changes, but it is in art and architecture that those revolutions are to be genuinely perceived by all. Indeed, while power changed hands, and both money and authority were given to the Church, it is the building programme initiated by Constantine, and the flourishing of Christian art, which would change our cities. Immediately after the victory at the Battle of the Milvian Bridge, Constantine sought to give Christians the architectural space to meet and pray. Many options were available to the emperor and his court. Constantine could have modified or adapted the faith to the existing sacred architecture, namely the Roman pagan temples. Indeed, if there already was an abundance of religious architecture (and art) present in the city of Rome, why did the emperor and his entourage not do so? Alternatively, he could have brought the Christian community to these temples after modifying and adapting them to Christian worship. If this was not his ideal choice, Constantine could have adapted other, non-religious, buildings to function as halls for

Christian worship. Finally, another option was to devise a radically new architecture for the newly recognised community. This would have been a logical choice. But the emperor did not do this; instead, he used a building type he knew all too well from his time in Trier (west Germany), namely the basilica. This type of building was the architectural expression of versatility, and although simple in form, it was multifunctional in its use. Oblong in shape, of rectangular form, with a central nave and an apse on one side, one or more pairs of side aisles separated by columns and a clerestory, the basilica was both large and multipurpose. Above all, because of its previous use as a court of law (and sometimes as a commercial exchange), it came with preconceived notions of authority and power, perceptions Constantine gladly provided to the Church. In essence, Constantine helped to establish the Church through a particularly generous building programme, especially in Rome, Constantinople and the Holy Land. And although one may study the various forms of palaeo-Christian architecture, the main building used for regular Christian gatherings was, from the Constantinian era onwards, the basilica, which in its many variations remains the prime choice for ecclesiastical architecture to this very day.

Can we single out any one specific event, or decision, be it political, legal, military, economic, architectural or religious, to build a strong argument for Constantine's status as a true historical giant? Perhaps his sudden conversion to Christianity would do the trick, although it was most likely a gradual process that took years. Nevertheless, it did lay the foundation for the changes about to come, and which would ultimately lead to the establishment of state Christianity later in the fourth century, and further into the various episodes of great tension between emperor and pope in medieval times, as well to the labyrinthine matrix of church-state relations in modern Western liberal democracies. On the other hand, I am strongly convinced that the full mosaic of Constantine's actions and decisions together progressively transformed the Roman world. His religious conversion and his legislative initiatives and architectural preferences should therefore be seen together with his selection of Byzantium as the new capital of the Roman Empire, modestly named Constantinople, and with other changes the emperor brought about. Such a multifaceted historical period is to be studied from an interdisciplinary perspective, by linking religion, politics, law, art and architecture, and by analysing the intersections and various influences of all the changes that took place. Perhaps that is the reason why Constantine remains a fascinating enigma for all of us, both experts and interested readers. There are various interpretations of the elements we know of his life, and few are truly unquestionable. Yet his overall impact on the development of Western civilisation is a certitude, and that makes Emperor Constantine very special.

2

Rome at the Dawn of the Fourth Century

Introduction

The Constantinian revolution did not happen in a vacuum. It was the answer to a long and multifaceted period of political, economic, medical and military instability which had started almost a century earlier, in AD 235, with the assassination of Severus Alexander by his own troops in Moguntiacum (present-day Mainz, Germany). During the fifty years that followed, up until AD 284, when Diocletian became emperor, the Roman world was hit by taxing challenges and problems on so many levels that this half-century would later be known as 'the imperial crisis'. Although our view of this transitional period of instability has recently become somewhat more nuanced, it remains the foundation for the various evolutions that were about to occur under the reign of Emperor Constantine.

The murder of Severus Alexander

Severus Alexander, most likely born in AD 208 in Phoenicia (corresponding to the coastal parts of Lebanon, Israel and Syria), became Emperor of Rome in AD 222, succeeding his cousin Elagabalus. His rule was particularly weak, and it is generally accepted that in reality his grandmother and mother were in charge – perhaps this is unsurprising in the case of a 14-year-old emperor. During his reign, many a Roman citizen lost faith in the government, mainly due to a series of bad decisions and military defeats. It is Alexander's pusillanimity that caused the empire to descend into half a century of severe trouble.

A crucial example is Alexander's peace deal with the German Alemanni tribe in AD 234, in reality an attempt to bribe them into peace, instigated by his mother and inspired by serious losses in previous military operations. This strategy created disappointment and havoc in army circles. The consequences would be catastrophic, for soon after the emperor fell victim to the swords of his own men. In the next few decades, at least thirty 'emperors' would claim leadership of the empire, most of them murdered by their own troops.

Military challenges

The military challenges Emperor Alexander faced were by no means exceptional. They would become a constant during the next half-century. Yet instead of preventing military intrusions from neighbouring armies on the northern and eastern borders of the empire, various army generals fought each other in a quest for power and control of the empire. Meanwhile, continuous raids by foreign tribes, such as the Alemanni, Carpians, Goths and Vandals, and pressure from attacks by Sassanid Persia, started to destabilise the empire, albeit temporarily. The costs were not only psychological; from a financial perspective, they were difficult to bear.

Yet Rome did not lose all of her battles during the imperial crisis; far from it. In AD 268, a Goth invasion was blocked by a Roman victory at the Battle of Naissus – the historic town where a few years later Helena would give birth to Emperor Constantine, and where more than a millennium later, in 1443, during the Battle of Niš, a Christian alliance would fight against the Ottoman Empire. And although Rome had suffered great losses, by AD 270, under the rule of Aurelian, a certain level of stability and military unity was re-established. For this, Aurelian would later be called *Restitutor Orbis* or 'Restorer of the World'.

Public health issues

Simultaneously with the vast array of military challenges, the Roman Empire faced large-scale medical issues. While the causes of the imperial crisis may be linked to various social, political and military decisions and circumstances, the devastating effects of the Antonin and Cyprian plagues and a series of other epidemics cannot be denied. To this day it is still unclear whether the Antonin plague, in the second century, and the Cyprian plague, almost a century later, were outbreaks of two different diseases (smallpox and measles), or if they were both smallpox. In any case, these public health problems were detrimental to the political foundations of the Roman Empire, producing a rising death rate and corresponding loss of manpower. Such issues had social and economic consequences, especially in combination with the other challenges the empire faced. Indeed, if the plagues and other public health challenges did not themselves cause the imperial crisis, they certainly did not contribute to its resolution, and diverted both energy and focus from other essential tasks and challenges.

Monetary problems

With a lack of serious, continuous leadership, and therefore an absence of strategic monetary policy, generals and emperors continued to debase the Roman currency. This, coupled with the expenses of the plague, civil wars and external military attacks, had a serious impact on the economy. Roman leaders reduced the silver content in coins, replacing it with bronze and copper. The main effect of this debasement was a hyperinflation that quickly got out of control. Ruined by economic chaos, vastly increased taxation and hyperinflation, local elites vanished. Roman society changed, and a new leader was urgently needed towards the last two decades of the third century. The Roman Empire, still at its peak only a century before, was now a sinking ship. Help would come from an unexpected source, in a strong and creative leader named Diocletian.

Diocletian's initiatives

Diocletian was born into a family of former slaves in AD 245. He joined the Roman army young, and gradually rose through the ranks. In AD 284 he ascended to the throne and became emperor of an empire in deep trouble. Although Aurelian had reunited it, the empire still had many issues to be dealt with. The borders were under constant attack, and economic challenges, in particular those caused by hyperinflation, were still ongoing. To tackle these issues and bring much-needed stability and a certain level of prosperity back to Roman society, Diocletian came up with an innovative idea: the tetrarchy.

Initially, he divided the leadership of the empire into two parts, with Maximian as his Caesar in AD 285 (this role could be seen as vice-emperor). In AD 286, Maximian would become an Augustus, Diocletian's co-emperor, and there was equilibrium between both emperors, who each governed his half of the empire. This arrangement is referred to as the diarchy ('rule of two'). Due to the many challenges facing the two leaders, in AD 293 the decision was taken to expand the imperial college with two more rulers, namely two Caesars, the first being Galerius and Constantius Chlorus. Each Caesar would from then on assist an Augustus.

These four leaders were spread geographically over the empire, in cities or military bases known as the tetrarchic capitals, Rome remaining the capital of the Roman Empire as a whole. In the East, Nicomedia (modern Izmit in Turkey) was Diocletian's political and military capital, while Galerius was stationed at Sirmium (modern Sremska Mitrovica in northern Serbia) on the Danube border. In the West, Maximian resided in Mediolanum (Milan, Italy), and his territory was Italy, Spain and Africa; and Augusta Trevorum (Trier) was the *polis* of Constantius Chlorus, strategically positioned near the Rhine border. Eboracum (York, England) was also a major centre for Constantius Chlorus.

After the discord and enmity between the numerous politico-military leaders during the crisis of the third century, it was crucial that the tetrarchic system was at least perceived to be a united empire (*patrimonium indivisum*). One of the consequences, from a numismatic perspective, was that all four tetrarchs would be depicted similarly on coinage, with the same characteristics and military costume.

The main advantage of both the diarchy in the first instance, and later the tetrarchy, was the presence of an emperor near every military conflict zone. This meant that emperors would be directly and simultaneously in control of the various military campaigns necessary to protect the empire's borders. This system had excellent results and brought important military victories.

When emperors Diocletian and Maximian reached their twenty-year jubilee in AD 305, they both quietly retired, the former to Split and the latter to southern Italy. They were replaced by their Caesars, Galerius and Constantius Chlorus. At the same time, two new appointments were made to assist them: Maximinus as Caesar to Galerius, and Flavius Valerius Severus as Caesar to Constantius. Yet this new tetrarchy would be neither long lasting nor harmonious; by AD 308 two of them had died (Constantius and Severus, who was murdered), and four men claimed the rank of Augustus in quick succession (Galerius, Constantine, Maximian and Maxentius). After AD 313, only two tetrarchs remained: Constantine in the West and Licinius in the East. The tetrarchic paradigm, so successful in its early days, slowly came to an end, not least due to internal discord and one man's insatiable individual quest for power. In 324, when Constantine defeated Licinius, the final verdict was given, and the last remainder of Diocletian's fine tetrarchic system was wiped away.

Diocletian had taken various initiatives beyond the tetrarchic system. When he saw the economic and monetary problems, he decided to issue the Edict on Maximum Prices (*Edictum de Pretiis Rerum Venalium*). It was a legal resolution that attempted to set a fixed price for goods, but Diocletian's project did not have the outcome wished for. An illegal market developed, some merchants and citizens used barter and prices were not easily controlled. By the end of Diocletian's reign, the edict was largely ignored. It would not be until the Constantinian reforms, a decade later, that the Roman economy stabilised.

Last but not least, Diocletian had decided to continue the persecutions of the Christians. The Christian communities had never been a popular group in the worldview of pagan Romans, and were seen as a suspect, secretive and segregated group that did not participate in the life of the Forum, nor in the ancient traditions and rituals of the empire, such as the public sacrifices, festivals and imperial cult. The Great Persecution, as it is called, under Diocletian's reign, was the last and most severe persecution of Christians in the Roman Empire. Perhaps this is why Diocletian has not been valued or studied as extensively as one would expect. He wanted to restore traditional Roman religion and values. Judaism was tolerated and, due to its great antiquity, exempted from persecutions. But the Christians were, in a sense, an easy prey: exotic, mysterious, relatively distinct from their Jewish origins and fairly new.

In February AD 303, Diocletian's edict against the Christians was issued. Its main objective was the destruction of both Christian scriptures and places of worship throughout the empire. Christians were discriminated against in judicial procedures, and those with administrative or political positions were deprived of their rank. Although Diocletian issued the edict with the objective of enforcing its rules 'without bloodshed', in practice capital punishment (especially being burnt alive) became a common method of persecution. During the summer of 303, a second edict was issued and its rules were harsher: the arrest and imprisonment of all bishops and priests were ordered. In November that year, the prisons so full of clergy men that regular criminals could not be sufficiently housed, Diocletian issued a third edict, in which it was stipulated that an imprisoned clergyman could be freed if he made a traditional sacrifice to the gods. Finally, in AD 304, a fourth and final edict of persecution was issued, ordering individuals to unite in the public forum to perform a collective sacrifice, failing which they were to be executed. Diocletian's persecutions were never systemically applied throughout the empire and there were various ways in which Christians could escape persecution, the simplest being to flee to more tranquil cities where the risk of persecution was lower.

After his abdication, and from his palace in Split, Diocletian saw many of his initiatives fail, but his major project, namely to prevent the empire from collapsing, as it was destined to during the imperial crisis of the third century, was a total success. Without a doubt, Diocletian saved the Roman Empire – for the time being at least.

3

Family Background
and Early Career

Family background

Constantine was born Flavius Valerius Constantinus in Naissus, modern-day Niš, in south-eastern Serbia, most likely on 27 February between AD 268 and 280. His exact year of birth is not known, not least because the emperor himself was vague about his age. Some historians would go along with this youthful image and place his birth in the eighties of the third century, yet it seems more likely that it is to be situated between AD 272 and 277.

His father, Flavius Constantius, was a native of Moesia, a Balkan region along the south bank of the Danube, who would later be known as Constantius Chlorus, due to his pale complexion. The socio-economic background of Constantius's family is not entirely clear; some see him as the offspring of a well-established family with clear aristocratic links, others would rather state his modest origins. In any case, he joined the army and made a quick progression through the ranks due to his outstanding service. Constantius was promoted to the position of *praeses* (governor) of the province of Dalmatia during the reign of Carus (AD 282–83). In AD 293, he was appointed Maximian's Caesar. His capital would be Augusta Treverorum ('City of Augustus in the land of the Treveri') – Trier.

Constantine's mother was Helena, a woman of mysterious background. Her family origins may be in Bithynia, in a city named Drepanum, but this is not entirely certain. It may be why Constantine renamed Drepanum Helenopolis after his mother's death in AD 330. Early sources mention her particularly modest background, being of low social status, possibly a stable maid. She is likely to have met Constantius while he was stationed in Asia Minor for a military campaign, but this cannot be argued with any degree of certainty. Nor do we know whether Helena was truly Constantius's wife or merely his concubine.

Constantius separated from Helena before the year AD 289, when he is known to have been married to Theodora, Maximian's daughter. This marriage finely illustrates the family bonds between the leaders of the tetrarchy. Following the split between his parents, Constantine and his mother Helena integrated into Diocletian's court. There, young Constantine received an education which can be described as both classical and intellectually stimulating: it is more than likely that he studied Latin literature, Greek and philosophy, interacting with the many philosophers who frequented the court.

Physical traits

Constantine's physical traits have been the object of many an analysis and to this day we are unsure what the emperor looked like. An eleventh-century Byzantine historian named George Kedrenos (Cedrenus) describes Constantine's looks: he had a thick neck, skin problems, little hair on his head and his beard was equally patchy. So notable was Constantine's neck that his nickname was 'bull-neck'. The description 'trachala' (from the Greek τράχηλος) meaning thick neck has a double signification: it relates both to physical appearance and an attitude which can be described as arrogant, pretentious, vain. The expression is still used, in various languages: in French, the saying to have 'le gros cou' has a similar meaning to the cognomen given to Constantine. Whether this nickname was aimed at Constantine's moral or physical traits remains a topic of debate, as portraits aren't always faithful to reality, and therefore neither numismatic analysis nor art historical studies can provide us with a final verdict.

Early military career

In AD 293 or 294, Constantine was appointed to his first military position: he took up the role of *tribunus*, as his father had at the start of his military career many years earlier. The military tribunes were junior officers, and the office was often a stepping stone for a fine career within the military or the Senate. That Constantine was appointed to this position at such a young age – he may still have been a teenager or at the most in his very early twenties – allows us to conclude that Emperor Maximian had confidence in the abilities and potential of the young man. That imperial foresight would soon be confirmed by the ambitious and gifted young officer Constantine became. In AD 298, he participated in the military campaign at the side of Galerius in Asia. In AD 301–02, he accompanied Diocletian in his military operations in Egypt, and we know he saw Memphis during his expedition. It might be there, at the remains of the magnificent Hout-ka-Ptah, the Great Temple of Ptah, that his first notions of the capital importance of sacred architecture originate. At that point, it was all but known what lay ahead in Constantine's future, and it was barely a decade later that he would start his own sacred building programme. Yet instead of magnificent pagan temples inspired by his Egyptian adventures, Constantine would opt to equip Christianity with impressive buildings, projecting a similar image of authority.

It is under Diocletian that Constantine was promoted to the rank of *tribunus ordinis primi*, tribune of the first order. And it is in Diocletian's company that Constantine must have witnessed the impact and influence of divine signs in the religious life of political and military leaders: the oracle of Apollo, which Diocletian had consulted for guidance, advised him to persecute the Christians.

4

Constantine and Christianity

Just before a decisive battle against Maxentius in the struggle for power over the Roman Empire, Constantine experienced a vision. This vision had assured him that he should conquer in the sign of the Christ, and his warriors carried Christ's monogram on their shields, though the majority of them were pagans. The opposing forces met near the bridge over the Tiber called the Milvian Bridge, and here Maxentius's troops suffered a complete defeat, the tyrant himself losing his life in the Tiber (28 October AD 312). From then on, Constantine 'grew close' to Christianity, although he only formally converted just before his death. Such a late conversion, however, does not mean that a private earlier conversion could not have taken place within his heart; extremely late conversions were not unusual as conversion wiped away all previous sins. This 'side' benefit was so important for many that they postposed the formal part of the conversion as long as possible, to be able to leave this earthly existence as pure as possible and to join the other world free from sin.

Within intellectual circles, one statement is agreed upon concerning the spiritual nature of Constantine: he 'turned' to Christianity during the second decade of the fourth century. As soon as we delve deeper into the details of what this 'turning' entails, namely how, when and, above all, why it happened, academic consensus vanishes into thin air. There are two approaches to the conversion of Constantine today: the literary and the contextual perspectives. Literary research implies analysing ancient texts to find indications of the veracity or sincerity of Constantine's conversion, and to use these texts as a foundation to develop a theory concerning the reasons and consequences of his religious preference. Contextual research has similar objectives but aims to deepen our understanding of a specific historical period, event, or figure through the analysis of art, architecture, social, cultural and religious customs and practices, economic data, legal traditions, and other non-literary sources of information.

Eusebius of Caesarea was an advisor to the Emperor Constantine after the defeat of Licinius. He was also a remarkably prolific defender of the Christian cause. A relatively large portion of his many works have been preserved, amongst them the *Ecclesiastical History*, the first surviving history of the Christian Church in a chronologically ordered account, based on earlier sources, complete from the period of the Apostles to his own epoch. In this text, we read:

Constantine, who was the superior both in dignity and imperial rank, first took compassion upon those who were oppressed at Rome, and having invoked in prayer the God of heaven, and his Word, and Jesus Christ himself, the Saviour of all, as his aid, advanced with his whole army, proposing to restore to the Romans their ancestral liberty.

And:

These [who obtained the victory from God] and the like praises Constantine, by his very deeds, sang to God, the universal Ruler, and Author of his victory, as he entered Rome in triumph. Immediately all the members of the senate and the other most celebrated men, with the whole Roman people, together with children and women, received him as their deliverer, their saviour, and their benefactor, with shining eyes and with their whole souls, with shouts of gladness and with unbounded joy. But he, as one possessed of inborn piety toward God, did not exult in the shouts, nor was he elated by the praises; but perceiving that his aid was from God, he immediately commanded that a trophy of the Saviour's passion be put in the hand of his own statue. And when he had placed it, with the saving sign of the cross in its right hand, in the most public place in Rome, he commanded that the following inscription should be engraved upon it in the Roman tongue: By this salutary sign, the true proof of bravery, I have saved and freed your city from the yoke of the tyrant and moreover, having set at liberty both the senate and the people of Rome, I have restored them to their ancient distinction and splendor.

Eusebius has often been accused of intentional falsification. According to many scholars, in his judgements of persons and facts, he is not entirely unbiased. The *Vita Constantini* (*The Life of Constantine*), most likely written by Eusebius, is a eulogy or panegyric, and therefore inadequate as a continuation of the *Church History*. It was unfinished at Eusebius's death. The *Vita* describes Constantine's relationship with God:

... and our own days prove it to be true, wherein Constantine, who alone of all that ever wielded the Roman power was the friend of God the Sovereign of all, has appeared to all mankind so clear an example of a godly life.

And God himself, whom Constantine worshipped, has confirmed this truth by the clearest manifestations of his will, being present to aid him at the commencement, during the course, and at the end of his reign, and holding him up to the human race as an instructive example of godliness. Accordingly, by the manifold blessings he has conferred on him, he has distinguished him alone of all the sovereigns of whom we have ever heard as

at once a mighty luminary and most clear-voiced
herald of genuine piety.

Another author, Lactantius, was a Christian and became
an advisor to Emperor Constantine and a tutor to his son.
His text *De Mortibus Persecutorum* is the first reference
to Constantine's vision at the Milvian Bridge. Lactantius
wrote that this was a divine intervention which guided
Constantine to victory over Maxentius.

Complementing the primary sources provided
by Eusebius, Lactantius and the author of the *Vita
Constantini* (if it was not Eusebius) is a vast array of
secondary literature. In these sources one can find many
theories concerning the emperor's conversion.

One of the first and most important contributions
to the analysis of Constantine's conversion is Jacob
Burckhardt's *The Age of Constantine the Great*.[1] Burckhardt
first points out that many attempts have been made to
penetrate the religious consciousness of Constantine
and to construct a hypothetical picture of changes in his
religious convictions. Burckhardt claims that, because of
his enormous ambition, Constantine, and any man for
that matter, who pictures himself standing in the midst
of a churchly community, is essentially unreligious. He
describes Constantine as a political opportunist invested
with a Christian mission. The monotheistic influence
came, according to Burckhardt, from Chlorus, his father.
Constantine's first religious act, or the first such act to

be noted, was his visit to the temple of Apollo at Autun in 308, just before his renewed attack upon the Franks. Burckhardt describes this event and places it in the context of Constantine's sun worship. He deduces from the inscription *SOLI INVICTO COMITI* ('To our comrade, the unconquered sun') that the personification of the sun as Mithras was implied and that Constantine had a deep connection with a special cult of Helios.

Burckhardt also points to two laws, of 319 and 321, post-dating the Edict of Milan, in which Constantine still recognises the pagan cult as existing of right, only forbidding occult and dangerous practices engaged in by magicians and *haruspices* (official diviners). Because Constantine tolerated conjurers of rain and hail, and requested responses from *haruspices* when public buildings were struck by lightning, Burckhardt seriously questions not only the validity of Constantine's conversion, but also the entire idea that he converted at all. He clarifies his theory by pointing to Zosimus, a fifth-century pagan writer who confirmed Constantine's consultation of pagan priests. Constantine's religious inconsistency indicated for Burckhardt that there was no sincere conversion; Constantine accepted the monogram of Christ as the emblem of his army and had the name of Jupiter erased from his triumphal arch, but retained the old gods on his coins, especially the sun god as his unconquerable companion. Burckhardt did not consider that some inconsistency is natural, and merely human.

Full consistency would represent a fundamentalism rarely seen in human nature, and would not imply greater sincerity – yet it is *praxis* that is crucial for Burckhardt, and from the acts and choices Constantine made, he cannot but conclude that the vagueness and ambiguity can only mean one thing: a so-called conversion that was really no such thing. He illustrates this by way of the construction projects of Constantine and his mother during the last decade of his life. While he clearly ornamented Palestine and various large cities around the empire with magnificent churches, Constantine was also building pagan structures, and temples, in the new Constantinople. Specifically, the temple and image of Tyche, the divine personification of the city, was intended to receive an actual cult. At the consecration of the city, certain occult pagan practices were demonstrably celebrated; the solemnities involved superstitions of all sorts, and this means, for Burckhardt at least, that Christianity was anything but present in the mind and spirit of Constantine. He argued that Constantine would not have presented such inconsistent, and at times illogical, behaviour had he really chosen a Christian way of life. Although some authors and believers have sought to interpret the actions and decisions made by Constantine as coherent with Christian theology or with the behaviour of a new convert, this is a hopeless strategy, and Burckhardt claims that we should not dedicate any energy to trying to justify the Christian nature of a man who was nothing but an overly ambitious pagan sun-worshipping conqueror.

A century before Burckhardt, Edward Gibbon had already tried to establish a rational critique of Constantine's conversion.[2] Gibbon distinguished three elements in the story of Constantine's conversion that need to be analysed. First, the standard; second, the dream; third, the celestial sign. He thus separated the historical, the natural and the marvellous parts of Constantine's story. Gibbon described the *labarum* as the principal standard that displayed the triumph of the cross (which he correctly describes as an instrument of torture in Rome). The *labarum* was a long pike intersected by a transversal beam from which hung a silken veil. On that beam was the mysterious monogram, simultaneously representing the figure of the cross and the initial letters of the name of Christ. Gibbon interpreted the *labarum* as a venerable but useless relic, a symbol that inspired courage and fear, but not a sign of the Christian nature of Constantine. He described the dream reported by Lactantius: Constantine was admonished to inscribe the shields of his soldiers with the celestial sign of God, the sacred monogram of the name of Christ; to execute the commands of Heaven; and his valour and obedience would be rewarded with a decisive victory on the Milvian Bridge. Lactantius wrote this text 1,000 miles away from Rome, and 1,000 days after the events at the Milvian Bridge, and this interval allows for doubts as to its credibility, for surely the emperor would have loved to listen to a marvellous tale that glorified him and promoted his designs.

Gibbon explains that the frequent repetition of miracles can inspire mankind to excogitate a reason for its very existence. Yet the dream of Constantine is, according to Gibbon, rather to be explained by the enthusiasm, and perhaps anxiety, of the emperor, as he was approaching the Battle of the Milvian Bridge. It seems rather a difficult argument to make, as delving deep into what really happened in a dream, if there really was a dream in the first place, is a psychological *post factum* analysis that is hardly realistic to execute many centuries later. It would imply analysing not only a subject dead for nearly two millennia, but also a situation and context from a psychological perspective which is already very complex when the subject is still alive and cooperating. Combine these difficulties with the fact that religious visions, or dreams about religious or theological events or situations, are in general a very intimate experience that are not easy to qualify with a modern scientific approach, and a recipe for failure is created. So questioning whether the dream, or vision of the symbol in the clouds, or a specific voice that spoke to Constantine, is real, is not the strategy to follow. Yet descriptions of these claimed events can help us contextualise and better grasp the situation and historical environment in which the conversion took place. A careful combination of both literary sources and contextual evidence, as illustrated by coins, architecture and legislation, seems to be the correct way to interpret whether Constantine was Christian, or whether there are enough elements pointing to the possibility of a latent Christianity.

Gibbon notes that the third element, namely Constantine's vision of a luminous cross above the meridian sun inscribed with the following words BY THIS CONQUER, is also unbelievable. At the moment of the vision, no clear religion was represented, but the night following the event, Christ is said to have appeared before Constantine and directed him to march with an assurance of victory against Maxentius and all his enemies. This story, like the previous account of the dream, is for Gibbon nothing more than the vanity of an emperor who felt flattered by the assurance that he had been chosen by Heaven to reign over the earth. This divine element explained his politico-military success, and as Gibbon saw it, the false piety of Constantine needed nothing more.

Henri Grégoire, a Belgian professor active in the first half of the twentieth century, gives us two elements to reflect upon in his *La Conversion de Constantin*.[4] He had initially declared that he would publish a magisterial opus on Constantine's life but it never materialised. The first critique he makes of the stories of Constantine's conversion is that the *Life of Constantine* is not a historical text but a romanticised panegyric. Furthermore, the *Life* is not a contemporary source for it is dated rather later than the events it describes (some say 337–40, at least a quarter of a century after the alleged conversion). Also, Grégoire points to the fact that the *Life* in its present form is a revised version published after the death of Eusebius which contains material that was not in the original. No writer in the fourth century knew the text. St Basil made no use of it, nor did St Gregory of Azianzus or St John Chrysostom. Most interesting is Grégoire's explanation of the dating of the story of Constantine's vision. He explains that a letter written by Cyril of Jerusalem, after 30 January 351, provides decisive evidence against the authenticity of the story or, at the very least, proves that the *Life* had not yet been published. At the beginning of 351, a bright meteor in the form of the cross is said to have appeared in the East, and contemporaries saw in this prodigy an omen of the decisive victory of Constantius II over Magnentius (the Battle of Mursa, 28 September 351). When Cyril of Jerusalem announced this prodigy to Constantius, he explained that the glorious vision with which he had been honoured elevated him well above his father Constantine. The latter had found the cross in the entrails of the earth, while Constantius had seen the salutary sign in the sky in broad daylight. This was supposed to be a much greater privilege, denied to Constantine. If this document dates from after 351, it raises great suspicion regarding the authenticity of the *Life of Constantine*. Grégoire furthermore points to the differences between Lactantius and Eusebius, and the stories of a dream that took place before the departure of the expedition for Rome (therefore in Gaul) and of a vision in the sky with a dream following shortly thereafter. It therefore seems that the *Life* does not confirm Lactantius's account of events, reason enough for Grégoire to doubt the whole conversion.

The second element brought forward by Grégoire is the monogram of Christ (☧). He explains that there is a striking similarity between the barred X placed in a laurel crown, which was one of the components of the Constantinian *labarum* (a distortion of *laureum* for *laureatum*, the standard with the *laurea*), and the numeral X in a laurel crown, which was the common symbol of the *vota* (the promise made to a deity, often in public ceremonies). According to Grégoire, nothing was more common on coins than the depiction of a shield on which the vows of the Roman people were inscribed. Long before the Battle of the Milvian Bridge in 312, Constantine's soldiers inscribed the number X of the decennalian vows on their shield. This sign differs only by an *iota* from the monogram of Jesus Christ which had been in use for quite a while in Asia Minor. Lastly, the sign soldiers inscribed on their shields was open for interpretation, for example the P could stand for *PLURIMA* or the whole formula could stand for *VOTA PUBLICA, VICTORIA PRINCIPIS PERPETUA* ('the everlasting victory of the emperor'). These inscriptions were rather common. Grégoire tells us that Constantine himself must have been struck by the manifold meanings of the symbol, which delighted the Christians but did not trouble the pagans, and is why Constantine allowed apparently Christianising monograms to be engraved on certain coins from 317 on.

It is thus clear, in Grégoire's eyes at least, that nothing allows us to speak about a conversion of Constantine, as these historical elements discredit the ancient primary sources we have, and the contextual evidence raises so much doubt that the possibility is nearly non-existent. We have to recognise the merits of Grégoire's approach but his doubts as to the primary sources and various interpretations given to Christian symbols are not convincing enough to reject the idea that Constantine underwent a sincere conversion. There may indeed have been an advantageous ambiguity concerning the symbol of the monogram of Jesus Christ. A similar example today could be a woman who wears a generic headscarf, made of certain fabrics and colours, in such a way that, in the eyes of an outsider, she could be Hasidic Jewish, Muslim or a member of a Christian order, a congregation or monastery. In other words, it is not the interpretation of believers or community members, or non-believers, that gives credibility or veracity to the faith of the believer – the *forum internum* is the only true witness of religious conversion. Various elements of external behaviour, the *forum externum*, can imply or signify a specific faith, but they do not exclude religious conviction entirely. And it is certainly not enough evidence to discredit the existence of a sincere religious conversion.

André Piganiol argues that the 'official' panegyrics delivered in 301, 311, 312 and 321 clearly indicate the primacy of the pagan vision of 310. Piganiol was one of a group of scholars who make the claim that Constantine was not the Machiavellian ruler depicted by Burckhardt and Grégoire. He saw the emperor rather as a simple and superstitious child of his time. Many authors who defend this view also integrate elements of syncretism into their theories to explain Constantine's combination of pagan or polytheistic rituals and Christianity.

Patrick Bruun was one of the first intellectuals to draw a picture of Constantine that was both profound and based on contextualised materials. His numismatic analysis is still the foundation for many scholars who approach to Constantine from a different angle, in this case, coinage. Bruun and his followers argue that by analysing the symbols that appeared on coins with the image of the emperor, conclusions can be drawn (to a certain extent). A complete analysis of Constantine's turn to Christianity cannot, of course, be made by focusing only on coinage or only on literary elements. It is the *ensemble* of knowledge that has come to us, many centuries later, that allows us to frame it. A full consensus will probably never be reached, but that is not just because we are discussing a religious conversion dating back to Late Antiquity. Modern conversions, and I refer to those that broader Western or European society tends to find difficult to accept, for example to Hasidic Judaism or Salafist Islam, or even to Hare Krishna or intense forms of Buddhism, are often rejected or frowned upon, and psychological statements or discriminatory remarks are easily made. It is indeed difficult if not impossible to truly measure the theological sincerity and conviction of another individual – are we even certain of being able to evaluate our own deepest convictions? Furthermore, the role and place of doubt are not minor elements in the process of religious conversion. Does sincere doubt, after a conversion, make the initial step towards a specific system of belief invalid? Does the political, social or other use of the advantages of membership of a cult or faith imply that the conversion was invalid? The answer might well be: no. True religious conversions would be impossible if the standard of piety were that high.

It seems that there are two mutually binding elements that are crucial to grasp the controversy: the (semi-) political use of religion and the widespread but rarely fully understood notion of syncretism, both in antiquity and modern times. First, the conceptual idea that a Roman emperor would specifically select the religion of a persecuted minority (no more than a small percentage of the population in the Roman Empire was Christian at the dawn of the fourth century) to strengthen his own political power and enlarge his influence on governmental and military matters seems implausible, yet this has been the prevailing opinion up to this day – although dissenting opinions have been and are today far-flung. Some authors, after discussing Constantine's conversion in detail, still select the option of a conversion inspired by politico-legal strategic incentives, despite knowing that Duchesne had already pointed out the following in 1907:

> We can not too much admire the naivety of some critics, who approach this imperial literature with the preconceived idea that an emperor could have no religious beliefs; that individuals like Constantine, Constantius, Julian, were in reality free-thinkers, who, for the purposes of politics and power, displayed such and such opinions. In the fourth century, freethinkers, if there were any at all, were rare birds, whose existence can not be presumed nor easily accepted.[5]

The position that is defended in *Histoire ancienne de l'Eglise* can be seen as quite rational indeed. It seems that the conversion has often been analysed from a deeply rooted anti-clerical perspective that leaves out any possibility of religious experience that does not comply with the traditions of post-Enlightenment religious practice. By this I mean that we should be careful of making two mistakes when contextualising Constantine's preference for Christianity: first, at the moment of his conversion, politics or, in a broader sense, governmental affairs, were not separated from other-worldly concepts or ideologies as one would believe they are in for example modern

France (with its politico-legal framework of *laïcité*) or in the United States (where the First Amendment to the Constitution excludes the establishment of one or more religions). The very idea of a 'wall of separation' between the spiritual and the political can theoretically be found in ancient sacred scriptures yet its practical implementation is very modern; it certainly was not a well-known concept of political theory in the third or fourth century. Therefore, the unnatural or inauthentic strategy of making Constantine's religious conviction a 'private' or family matter without it interfering with his political, legal or military duties or without it having any impact in the realms of governmental power would be suspicious. It would not have been a natural way of dealing with his new belief. The implementation of measures that are logical consequences of this new belief (such as, but not limited to, the Edict of Milan and various other innovative rules to either protect or advantage Christians or Christian communities), which, according to some, should raise eyebrows, is in fact a logical consequence of the sincerity of Constantine's conversion, as only the opposite behaviour would have been really revolutionary.

The second point, concerning the disagreement on the conversion of Constantine, is influenced by syncretism. This syncretism is highly related to the use of religion in politico-strategic affairs and socio-ritual traditions, as there were no clear boundaries between religion and government, or between various religious traditions.[6] The very notion of theological syncretism was rather different in Late Antiquity from what current scholars would define as religious syncretic practices. Then, syncretism was a logical step after having conquered new territories or communities; the local gods were simply added to the existing portfolio.

While current scholarship would describe syncretism as the lateral, bilateral or multilateral influence of a religious worldview on another, this seems like a light version of syncretism when one might speak of fusion or deep syncretism between various faiths in Late Antiquity. Current doctrines of religious liberties, legal and political scholarship on fundamental rights, do not mention multiple religious identities. It seems that the paradigm that an individual has one religion, and can be categorised by this religion, is standard thought. Only mentioned on the fringes of scholarship, a polyparadigmatic approach, whereby religious practice is no longer seen as a sort of serial monogamy in which religious identity is always singular though with potential to change (although even the very nature of religious conversion is controversial in legal and interdisciplinary scholarship), is all too rare. Within the field of modern religious anthropology, and religious studies in general, this area is promising yet lagging behind a phenomenon of society and philosophico-religious reality that has been with us since long before the Graeco-Roman world. Yet when studying these concepts, it is particularly interesting to look at the various practices of Greek and Roman syncretism.

In the framework of Constantine's conversion to Christianity, it therefore seems essential to place the choice of a new faith in the context of a syncretism that was widespread and natural. His integration of elements of previous religious practices, and his decision not to abolish his sun worshipping to focus entirely on Christian monotheism in general and discipleship of Jesus of Nazareth in particular, is therefore the clue to understanding the sincerity of Constantine's conversion. Analysing Constantine's conversion from a syncretic perspective is far from new, yet I believe that the division between scholars can be bridged by framing the question of the veracity of his conversion in a different light by using syncretism as one major element but not the only one. Combining a critical reading of the primary literary sources and these syncretic contextualising notions with external elements such as architecture, numismatics, art, urban planning, law, economics and other disciplines, allows for a more nuanced picture – a picture that gives us a more or less clear indication that Constantine was sincere in his quest towards Christianity, without denying the secular uses of the Christian religion.

5

Political and Legal Innovations under Constantine's Reign

Immediately after turning to Christianity, in AD 312, Emperor Constantine sought to bring changes to the politics and laws of the Roman Empire, in a more autocratic way than most emperors before him. Some of these new measures were clearly inspired by his choice of the Christian faith, others are less clearly linked to religion. In various instances, one may debate whether the texts produced by Constantine were letters, edicts or laws; in any case, their impact was often the same.

The most important primary source for analysing Constantinian legislation is the Codex Theodosianus or Theodosian Code, initiated under Emperor Theodosius II in the fifth century as a compilation of Roman imperial laws. The fact that the Theodosian Code starts with Constantine in AD 312 is why we still have a good view on the legislative initiative taken by the emperor. Besides the Theodosian Code, very few sources are available: one papyrus, a few inscriptions, a number of letters (in particular those collected by Eusebius of Caesarea) and two collections of law, namely the *Collectio Sirmondiana* (named after Jacques Sirmond) and the *Fragmenta Vaticana*.

The Edict of Milan

The Edict of Milan is one of Constantine's first and most important legal initiatives. It is a short text which guarantees the protection of religious freedom throughout the Roman Empire. The edict, in fact a letter, was the record of an agreement reached in Mediolanum (Milan) in February AD 313 by the two emperors: Constantine, who was then controlling the western empire, and Licinius, who was in charge of the eastern territories. They formally agreed to change policies regarding the Christians, thereby confirming, and supplementing, a previous edict of toleration that had been issued by Emperor Galerius in AD 311. Is this an example of international human rights law *avant la lettre*? Up to a certain point, and in the eyes of the Christian communities of the time, it certainly was a welcomed evolution, yet one can hardly speak of the conceptual notion of religious liberty as it is known today. Persecutions were in AD 313 something of a not-so-distant past, and the edict merely formally established the liberty to practise any faith. It did, however, specifically mention Christianity, and indeed should be interpreted as targeting the Christian communities:

And thus by this wholesome counsel and most upright provision we thought to arrange that no one whatsoever should be denied the opportunity to give his heart to the observance of the Christian religion, of that religion which he should think best for himself, so that the Supreme Deity, to whose worship we freely yield our hearts, may show in all things His usual favor and benevolence.[7]

The edict changed the politico-legal framework in which the Christians operated, it ignited spectacular changes in Roman society for suddenly Christians were formally allowed to practise their faith in the open. This created circumstances in which the demographic evolution of the Christian communities would fast become exponential. Furthermore, in this new context of political recognition, the need arose for a building programme to house the Christian communities, who could now gather freely and unite in grander architectural spaces than the house churches.

It is particularly challenging to theorise on what would have happened to the early Christian communities if the Edict of Milan had not established their freedom to worship. Yet the impact of Constantine legalising the Christian faith remains a major milestone not only in the history of early Christianity, but of the Western world as we know it. Together with Constantine's conversion, the edict was the trigger which allowed the many changes in Roman society under Constantine's reign. But the edict did not make the traditional religions illegal; nor did it make Christianity the state religion. This would happen later that century with the Edict of Thessalonica in AD 380.

The *audientia episcopalis*

In AD 318, just five years after granting religious freedom to all and to Christians in particular, Constantine the Great modified the Roman legal system in a way which would have consequences so significant that they would lay the foundation for much of the conflictual relations between church and state in the middle ages, and up to this very day. He proposed the concept known as the *audientia episcopalis*, which would from then on allow bishops to replace secular Roman judges in a certain number of legal proceedings. An *audientia episcopalis* would be granted even if only one of the parties demanded a case to be brought before a bishop. Although the bishops did not become Roman officials, they did become *de facto* judges, hence acquiring the privilege to settle disputes, and the power to do so with authority, as initially no appeals to their decisions were possible.

The *audientia episcopalis* was not the only privilege Constantine accorded to members of the clergy; church lands were not subject to tax, and various other monetary and fiscal policies were created to favour the clergy. But with the conferral of secular judiciary power came the perception of great authority; the church was adapting to this change, from being persecuted merely a decade earlier, to being part of the state establishment, a new paradigm. The *audientia episcopalis* and the very notion of clergy members dealing with legal disputes and thus pronouncing judgements on matters of secular life, is the crux in the Constantinian shift. It goes much further than merely recognising the *privilegium fori*, which is an application of the principle of trial by one's peers, in this case spiritual peers (Christians), rather it is a singling out of the Church to share worldly power and privileges which would create the difficult matrix of church-state relations. These latter are, in most jurisdictions, still entangled and/or in a delicate equilibrium to this day.

The *dies solis*

The Jewish custom of celebrating a weekly day of rest, the Sabbath, from sunset on Fridays until nightfall on Saturdays, was still practised by Christian communities in the first few decades of the fourth century, although some were already observing it the day after Saturday.

On 7 March AD 321, less than a decade after he turned to Christianity, Emperor Constantine accelerated that gradual evolution, by issuing a decree that made Sunday the day of rest and worship, even for those who were not Christian:

> On the venerable day of the Sun let the magistrates and people residing in cities rest, and let all workshops be closed. In the country however persons engaged in agriculture may freely and lawfully continue their

pursuits because it often happens that another day is not suitable for grain-sowing or vine planting; lest by neglecting the proper moment for such operations the bounty of heaven should be lost.[8]

The ambiguity of this innovation, namely the fact that Sunday would be the Christian day of rest, but also a day in the honour of the Sun, is typically Constantinian. It remains a mystery whether the emperor sought thus to satisfy both Christian and pagan communities, or whether he had other, possibly personal, objectives. What is certain is that the *dies solis* was one more step in the establishment of a clear Christian identity, separate from its Jewish origins.

Fiscal policy

Constantine made sure that citizens were protected against wrong fiscal decisions; recourse to appeal was made possible and tax money which was not due could be returned to the citizen making the complaint. Furthermore, those owing outstanding taxes could no longer be incarcerated. Yet he also created new taxes, not least the *collatio lustralis*, which was levied every five years upon trade and business. Others, in particular the Church and its clergy, were to be exempted from tax, or would pay minimal taxes. Similarly, between AD 320 and 328, five laws regarding the pensions and taxes of veterans were enacted. Thanks to their loyal service in the military they would be exempted from certain taxes and municipal charges.

Constantine allowed for certain tax remissions; a typical example is the French city of Augustodunum (Autun), which received an almost 25 per cent cut in its taxes, and also saw its arrears cancelled.

In general, Constantine perpetuated the extremely heavy tax burdens which were necessary for the costly imperial projects he had initiated, but which alienated the Roman population and created widespread hostility to the state, mainly due to the destructive impact it had on the middle class.

Other legislative innovations

Constantine was an active legislator, and his legal initiatives were not limited to religious phenomena. He was especially active in family and criminal law. Within family law, he focused on the protection of both patrimonial assets and children, and the very institution of marriage itself. Divorce would be more difficult when the demand came from one party only. A long list of legislative innovations was proclaimed, dealing with topics such as testamentary law, tax law, forcible abduction, slavery, the law of sale, and co-habitation of women and slaves. Indeed, the law of persons was of major concern to the emperor.

For example, the consequences for female Roman citizens who had amorous encounters with slaves were drastic: the death penalty was possible for the woman, and the slave would be burnt alive. In general, though, legal protection for women and children was reinforced, especially with two laws specifically dealing with the abandonment of children and the abduction of girls, which up until this point in time had not been punishable. This was revolutionary and can perhaps be seen as one example of the Christian influence on the Roman legal system. Yet the trade in children, namely parents selling their offspring under the pressure of creditors, remained a sad practice that even later laws could not fully eradicate.

Constantine was equally preoccupied with the functioning of the judiciary, and he created laws in AD 325 and 326 to protect citizens from unethical lawyers, whose fees could, in some instances, be revoked.

Criminal law in the Roman system was known for its severe punishments. The various traditional sanctions remained in place: exile, death, torture, forced labour. The death penalty was pronounced for homicide, adultery, counterfeiting money and black magic. In some areas Constantine seems to have implemented a more humane system of punishment as he abandoned sanctions such as gladiator fights and in some instances crucifixion, although this must fairly quickly be nuanced as he introduced other, equally barbaric punishments, for example the pouring of molten lead into the mouth and the removal of the tongue. Perhaps some Christian influence can be seen in the fact that the face could no longer be branded by a hot iron: human faces were not to be disfigured as they were fashioned in the likeness of God; only the feet could be marked.

Some of Constantine's legal innovations show that he was not afraid to incorporate so-called 'vulgar law' (i.e., popular legal concepts). In this sense, the emperor created a framework within which the law could evolve with society's demands and which allowed it to abandon some of the traditional principles of Roman law. This was a major change from Diocletian's attitude to the law; he can be seen as the very last defender of the system of pure classical Roman law. One cannot state that Constantine abandoned classical law or classical jurisprudence altogether for they certainly remained in force. Progressive and open to oriental and Christian influences he certainly was, but to what degree remains a topic of fierce academic debate.

Theology

9

Introduction

In the early fourth century, the spiritual landscape in the Roman Empire consisted of an official paganism with its diverse politico-religious rituals on the one hand, and a number of other cults and faiths on the other, Judaism and Mithraism being merely two examples. When Constantine was introduced to the Christian Church, and its internal pluralism and enmities, he may have been guided by his political leitmotiv 'one empire, one God'. Yet instead of finding a united church, he immediately faced two major issues which created divisions in the various Christian communities: Donatism and Arianism. Although it remains unclear to what extent he was personally involved in settling these internal Church disputes, we know that he spared no effort to create at the very least the framework in which the Church could find harmony, peace and especially unity.

The Donatist controversy concerned a group of Christians living in North Africa. During the persecution of Emperor Diocletian in the first decade of the fourth century, a number of Christians had renounced their faith in order to survive, and although most of the Church was ready to welcome them back into the community after the persecutions had ended, the Donatists had a different, more rigorous perspective. They strictly refused to accept the sacraments from, and did not recognise the theological authority of, those priests and bishops who had renounced their faith during the persecution. The controversy caused great division in various towns in North Africa; there was tension, a great deal of unrest and even violent riots. Constantine made several attempts to restore unity, condemning the Donatists as heretics at the Council of Arles in AD 314, and publishing an edict in AD 317, but he failed. By AD 321 Constantine granted tolerance and pleaded for patience with the Donatists. The Donatist schism and internal discord in the Church would continue for several centuries.

Nicaea

Constantine also intervened in deep theological debates and one of his most impactful interventions, relatively soon after the promulgation of the Edict of Milan, was the organisation and implementation of the first ecumenical council[9] of the Christian Church in Nicaea in AD 325. The earliest extant uses of the term 'ecumenical' for a council are the *Life of Constantine*, produced around 338, which states σύνοδον οἰκουμενικὴν συνεκρότει ('he convoked an Ecumenical council'); Athanasius's letter *Ad Afros Epistola Synodica* of 369; and the letter of 382 sent to Pope Damasus I and the Latin bishops by the First Council of Constantinople. Constantine, inspired by the synod led by Hosius of Córdoba in the Eastertide of 325, organised the council and invited all 1,800 bishops of the Christian Church (not all of whom attended).[10] The council did not create the conceptual notion of a 'divine Jesus' as is commonly understood, but it did settle, to a certain extent, the debate within the early Christian communities regarding the divinity of Christ; this was the Arianist debate. The council affirmed and defined what it believed to be the teachings of the Apostles with regards to who Christ is: namely that Christ is the one true God in deity, with the Father, thereby rejecting Arianism (which denies the divinity of Christ). Jesus Christ was described as 'God from God, Light from Light, true God from true God'. He was said to be 'begotten, not made', asserting his co-eternalness with God and confirming it by stating his role in the Creation. He was said to be 'from the substance of the Father', in direct opposition to the position of Arianism. Eusebius of Caesarea ascribes the term ὁμοούσιος, or consubstantial, 'of the same substance' (as the Father), to Constantine who may have chosen to exercise his authority on this particular point.

More importantly, the council achieved truly major results with regards to the doctrine and organisation of the early Church. It resulted in the first uniform Christian declaration of faith, called the Creed of Nicaea or Nicene Creed. A creed is a doctrinal statement of correct belief, created in a quest for orthodoxy, to align the Church in major theological matters. Especially in a time of internal conflict, a creed helps to align the various groups of believers. In the Nicene Creed, the term 'consubstantial' is used to affirm the divine nature of Christ, clarifying that the Arian dispute had been settled (in theory).

The council is also historically extremely significant as it was the first undertaking to create common ground, a theological consensus, through an assembly that was supposed to represent the whole of Christendom. The debates were not limited to Christology and the divine nature of Jesus. An important issue was the exact place of the Easter celebration in the ecclesiastical calendar.

Another topic of debate was the validity of baptism performed by heretics. Although there were various approaches to the very notion of religious identity in Late Antiquity, it is clear that in the context of a growing division between orthodoxy and heresy, the importance of baptism was not to be underestimated.[11] In Paul's letter to the Romans, we read, 'We were therefore buried with him through baptism into death in order that, just as Christ was raised from the dead through the glory of the Father, we too may live a new life' (Romans 6:4). This significant passage shows the importance of baptism in the life of the early Christians, from a soteriological point of view, but also in a broader perspective for baptism can be seen as the entry to Christian identity; it becomes the essential *rite de passage* to fully 'being Christian'.

Although the Bible is far from silent on the topic of baptism,[12] various interpretations have been given. On the controversial question of whether infant or adult baptism was the intention or strategy to follow; on the necessity of water; on the location or ceremony that was necessary or to be wished for (for example, specific declarations or the signing of a document): all these socio-theological issues continued to be debated, showing that baptism was used not just for the ritual aspect of welcoming new converts, but more and more for defining who was a member of the Christian community, and who was not. In this scenario, it is essential to understand that it was not only the rebirth, or the forgiveness of sins, that was the main point in performing the ritual of baptism. Within the sociocultural context of the development of early Christianity, the initiation procedure was slowly becoming essential to separate outsiders from insiders. This inclusion-exclusion perspective, namely 'us' versus 'them', and the creation of a certain kind of conformity while defining what was to be seen as heretic, was an element of boundary-setting in antiquity (and would continue to be throughout Late Antiquity – and even up to this day), and baptism, although a valid ritual from a theological perspective, was one of the ways in which this was done. Therefore, it is no surprise that at Nicaea the question of the validity of baptism by heretics was raised.

Canon law

A foundation for Canon law[13] was developed at the Council of Nicaea, and a list of twenty canons (laws) issued by the council survive, besides the famous Nicene Creed.

The feast of Easter is linked to the Jewish Pesach and the Feast of Unleavened Bread. As Christianity was still establishing its own distinct religious identity, entirely separate from Judaism, some Christians sought to establish their own date of Easter. This was quite similar to the selection of Sunday as the weekly day of rest, distinct from the Jewish Sabbath. At the Council of Nicaea it was decided that the computation of the date of Easter would henceforward be a purely Christian matter and that one would no longer rely upon the Jewish calendar.

Separate from the Donatist and Arian disputes, another issue of internal discord was to be dealt with at the council, namely the Meletian schism. Similar to the Donatists, the followers of Miletius, Bishop of Lycopolis, who went by the name the Church of the Martyrs, were a sect concerned with those Christians re-entering the Church after having forsaken their faith in the persecutions. During the Council of Nicaea there was an attempt to make peace with the Meletians and it was decided that Miletius could remain Bishop of Lycopolis. The efforts to bring unity with the Meletians were unsuccessful, and although Miletius would die fairly rapidly after the council, his followers continued as a sect until the fifth century.

More importantly, the council created what is now seen as proto-Canon law, as it laid the foundation for the development of the internal legal system in the Church. Twenty church laws were proclaimed, the 'canons', which deal with an eclectic mix of internal church issues. Agreement was reached on a variety of doctrinal and internal structural matters, from the establishment of a minimum term for catechumens, to the way bishops were to be ordained (the presence of at least three provincial bishops and confirmation by the metropolitan bishop would be necessary); from the specific authority of the patriarchs of Alexandria, Antioch and Rome, to the declaration of the invalidity of baptism performed by Paulian heretics.

Constantine

Constantine's own role remains a matter of dispute. He organised the council, invited the bishops, arranged for the financing of travel and lodging, and gave the council a worthy venue at the Bithynian city of Nicaea (now İznik, Bursa province, Turkey). His objective seems to have been clear: to eradicate discord and enmity, and stimulate harmony and unity. He did speak to the audience of bishops and their assistants, but it does not seem to have been the case that he imposed his own theological paradigms; rather, he facilitated the discussions which led to agreements, and used his influence to make sure consensus was reached. It would have been rather strange to have an emperor, still very much involved in pagan rituals, deciding upon theological and spiritual matters internal to the Church; even if Constantine had sincerely turned towards Christianity in October 312, he did not formally convert until 337, and although it was quite traditional for individuals to become Christian without an immediate baptism, one might ask whether Constantine really was a Christian when he convened the first major ecumenical council in 325. That paradox, a pagan-Christian emperor seeking to reunite both the empire and the Church, organising grand church meetings and creating the context for doctrinal declarations, yet still involved in paganism, will likely remain a mystery unsolved.

Misunderstandings

Various misconceptions have arisen with regards to the actions and decisions taken by both the council and Emperor Constantine. The development of the biblical canon was a centuries-long process and the Council of

Nicaea did not decide which books were to be included and which excluded. Nor was the notion of the Trinity decided at the council, only the divisive question concerning the divine nature of Christ was dealt with. At the council, no bibles were commissioned – Constantine would order fifty bibles in 331 but there is no conclusive evidence pointing to the emperor selecting which books should be included in or omitted from those bibles.

The canon which deals with the authority of the patriarchs of Alexandria, Antioch and Rome remains a source of disagreement between various modern-day churches and theologians, even within the Roman Catholic Church. Some argue that the supreme leadership of the Bishop of Rome, as pope and jurisdictional head of Christendom, was decided at the council; others, more in line with the canon cited above, see the Bishop of Rome as an influential figure, but not one with authority over bishops in other regions.

7

Constantine's Building Programme

Introduction

Constantine may have been active as a legislator, but his architectural programme also, or even more so, left a lasting legacy. Beside early Christian art, it is architecture that shows the most perceptible of all changes to the Roman world of the fourth century. Where legal and spiritual evolutions certainly have a major impact, architecture can be experienced, touched and seen, thereby creating specific emotions and perceptions. By giving the Christian communities not only the freedom to practise their faith but also the funding and infrastructure to organise their worship, Constantine radically changed the sacred landscape. From Trier to Rome, from Constantinople to Jerusalem: during his three-decade reign, Constantine enthusiastically built churches all over his empire, in various shapes and forms, although some constant architectural paradigms are crucial to palaeo Christianity.

Traditionally, when analysing the evolution, and transformation, of sacred architecture in the early Christian environment of Late Antiquity, one fairly quickly asks why the basilica was chosen as the categorical expression of the newly recognised faith. One thereby reflects on the various architectural possibilities that were available at the time, and carefully ponders why this or that specific form was *not* chosen, and why the basilica became the *ne plus ultra* of early (and many later) Christian church architectures.

Yet the very first question we need to ask is of a different order. If there was already an abundance of religious architecture (and art) present in the city of Rome, why did the emperor and his entourage not modify, or adapt, the faith to the existing architecture, instead of the other way round? Christianity's integration into the Roman religious and social landscape would perhaps have been much simpler if the faith had been transformed to fit the architectural infrastructure already present. Several strong theological assumptions prevented Constantine and the early Christian communities of Rome from doing so.

First, the idea behind Christianity was not merely to sacrifice and offer gifts to the divine, as in the Roman tradition, where religious ritual somehow implied a contractual *do ut des* attitude (in the sense of 'we offer sacrifice and in return the gods are favourable to us'). Christianity was above all a participatory experience:

the faithful came together to celebrate, pray and to be full members of the congregational service. Where in traditional Roman religion, the temple was used to honour the gods, Christian churches were much more, and proactive participation of all Christians, not merely the priest, was essential. Therefore, one can only conclude that it would have been necessary to modify the nature of Christianity at its very core to adapt it to the Roman temples. The emperor certainly did not want to take unnecessary risks, either by going against the Christian communities in changing their *praxis*, or by 'conquering' the temples for worship of a very different kind. In other words, the nature of the Christian faith, with its interactive, participatory and collective elements, was so thoroughly different that changing it to conform with the previous polytheistic religious practices of Rome would have required changing its very identity. Using non-modified temples was therefore not an option, at least not when Constantine was emperor – the strategy had to be different, and form would follow function and theological understanding: the architecture of Christianity had to suit the typically Christian way of worshipping, even though Christian worship was also influenced by the ultimate strategic choice of building policy. Later on, several pagan temples were adapted to Christian use, the Pantheon being a fine example.

A second possibility, having realised that merely moving Christianity, either straight or in a modified form, into pagan temples was not a sound option, was to bring the Christian community to these temples nonetheless – but after modifying and adapting them to Christian worship.

This might have been a rather radical solution, first because of the politico-social context, and second because of the architectural impact. Indeed, one can only imagine the consequences of such an act in Roman social life: claiming temples which were still very much in use, and which basically were the *de facto* place and form of religious worship, would not have made for an easy entry of Christianity in broader Roman society. Let us not forget that Christianity was merely tolerated at the beginning of the second decade of the fourth century; the Edict of Milan gave freedom to Christians, but not the power to do whatever they wanted. They were not ruling the empire, Christians were just able to live their faith in the open. Although this would gradually change over the next few decades, pagan ritual was not to be discarded at this point. In that sense, Christianity and paganism were coexisting and sharing the religious landscape – so there was no question of conquering each other's terrain during the early stages of Christianity's move above ground. Second, the nature of Christian worship was so thoroughly different from the ancient pagan rituals that extreme forms of modification and grand architectural works would have been necessary. This would likely have been perceived as shocking and somehow blasphemous to the Roman gods and (obviously even more so from a practical point of view) to those who led, and practised, the Roman religion. We are here speaking of the gods who, after all, had done so many great things for Rome's leaders and population.

Another option would have been the adaptation of other, non-religious, buildings. The variety in Roman architecture was great enough and several choices would have been possible. Sacred space that would have focused more on the communal settings, for example in a circular area instead of a long nave leading up to the apse, could have been an option, similar to the form decided on for baptisteries. We cannot declare with certainty why such a route was not preferred.

Apart from choosing and adapting existing religious buildings, or non-religious buildings, a further option was to develop a radically new architecture for the newly recognised community. This would have been a logical step. The Christian community was small, and architecturally relatively unestablished. It was given a new chance, a rebirth, when Constantine chose to recognise and privilege it with politico-legal and financial measures beyond its wildest expectations. With these new times, a new architectural concept would have meant a break with the past, a new dawn for the faithful communities which had been persecuted and lived under harsh conditions for so long. As the tides were finally turning, and as Constantine had wisely decided to construct the new buildings for the Christian Church on the outer borders of the city, where space was available and new constructions would not have drawn too much suspicion, he might as well have allowed for a creative, innovative architectural perspective on sacred space.

Yet he did not. The basilica, a long building of considerable size, with its central nave, two or more side aisles, clerestory and apse, was chosen – over and over again, from Trier to Rome, and in other parts of the empire, including Jerusalem and Constantinople, albeit, in first instance, with slight variations.

Trier

One of Germany's oldest towns, if not the oldest, Trier was of major importance both before and during Constantine's reign. Augusta Treverorum, as the city was called in Latin, became a seat of Roman administration in the first century; it was a centre of trade and had a strategic military importance. Emperor Constantine resided here for ten years, until AD 315. Two Constantinian buildings are particularly noteworthy: the twin basilica and the audience hall.

The twin basilica was a huge complex, constructed between 326 and 348, situated in the palace district in the north-eastern part of the city. It consisted of two equally large halls, both of which had an atrium and a narthex at their west end.

The Aula Palatina, known as the Konstantinbasilika in German, is nowadays used as a church, open for the faithful and tourists alike. It is an impressive brick structure of oblong form and with a particularly high ceiling. It was used as the throne hall, or audience hall, of the Roman emperor, until the city of Trier was attacked by Germanic tribes. The basilica is a clear example of the magnanimity the Romans wanted to express in the architectural framework for the Roman emperor to receive guests. First, one notices its sheer size, which is accentuated by small details, such as the central windows in the apse, which are slightly smaller than the adjacent ones, thereby enhancing the impression of length. The basilica is a rectangular building 220ft long, 90ft wide and 98ft tall. The semi-circular apse is vast, and the basilica is the largest surviving single-room structure from Roman times. The basilica now has an austere atmosphere, as it is 'naked', its bricks visible inside and out – although here and there on the exterior walls one can still see some spots covered with plaster and paint, in particular close to the windows, as used to be the case for the whole exterior. The interior of the building was richly decorated in Roman times, with colourful marble inlays, golden mosaics and statues, and a hollow-floor heating system created an agreeable interior temperature.

The Aula Palatina was built around AD 310, and therefore predates what we currently identify as Constantine's Christian building programme. It gives us a sense of what Constantine considered an appropriate format to convey the grandeur in which Roman leadership wanted to be perceived. It is this perception of authority, power and grandeur that we will encounter again later, when Constantine combines his architectural experience of the past with the legal heritage associated with the basilica form.

Rome

Although they can be classified as merely one type of early Christian architecture, episcopal basilicas represent in a way the essence of the transformation of sacred space in Classical and Late Antiquity. They are highly visible, very symbolic structures, which welcome the faithful for regular religious gatherings. The first of the Constantinian basilicas seems to have been the Lateran.

The name of the Basilica Lateranensis relates, as we shall see, to the location of the building. Yet it was also named the Basilica Constantiniana after its founder, and Basilica Salvatoris as it was consecrated to the Saviour. The name by which it is now known, basilica S. Iohannis (San Giovanni in Laterano) dates back to the Early Middle Ages and seems to be linked to the magnificent baptistery which stood just next to the basilica. (It still stands there, although it is now physically linked to the basilica.) Constantine had probably founded the church, in light of his victory at the Milvian Bridge, as a consecration to the Salvator. Yet quite soon the topographical name Lateranum appeared, and Basilica Constantiniana was common in the fifth century. Only after AD 600 do we see 'Basilica Salvatoris' being used.

In the *Vita sancti Silvestri* (also known as *Actus Silvestri*) the founding of the church is narrated – incorrectly – in detail.[15] In reality, it was almost immediately after the Battle at the Milvian Bridge that Constantine initiated the project that would become the Basilica Salvatoris. The grounds of the *equites singulares*, who had fought Constantine at the side of Maxentius, were from that point on destined for use by the Church. The buildings were named after the Laterani, an ancient Roman family who lived in a part of Rome called Laterano, which we cannot identify, during the First Empire. A basilica of considerable size was destined for use by the Bishop of Rome and his community. Simultaneously, a *baptisterium* and *episcopium* would be erected. The basilica and baptistery were constructed after Constantine's successful power struggle in AD 312 and before the founding of Constantinople in AD 324. The basilica was a radically new construction: on top of the former barracks of his enemy's imperial guard, which were demolished to a level of 1.10m above ground. The surrounding buildings were to be left untouched, hence the difference in ground level; the baptistery is a considerably lower level than the basilica. There is still a debate within academic scholarship whether the baptistery was built *ex novo* or whether it was established in the circular room of an existing *domus*. This baptistery would remain until late in the fourth century, the only one in *intra-muros* Rome.

The church was to be the liturgical seat of Rome, one and indivisible – even after the founding of the titular churches. It was to be a sacred space for grand Christian celebrations at regular intervals during the religious year, and new bishops would be ordained within its walls. It was, in a sense, a safe area, quite distant from the pagan rituals and senatorial families, as it was separated from regular city life by green pastures. It remains a striking fact that Constantine erected a Christian church on the grounds of the former headquarters of his rival's principal military force.

Earthquakes, fires and many restorations prohibit a full history of the building – even Krautheimer and Corbett were not able to fully grasp its earliest history. Yet we do have a certain level of knowledge of what resides underneath the accomplishments of Della Porta, Borromini, Galilei and Vespignani, and research has far from exhausted the subject. The original form and proportions of the Lateran were discovered during excavations carried out by Josi (1934–37) and Krautheimer and Corbett (1957–58).

Constantine's basilica is a rectangular structure with a longitudinal axis, a nave which was illuminated with clerestory windows and double side aisles. Its semi-circular apse is oriented to the west; its façade with the main entrance to the east, towards the rising sun. There are no traces of an atrium, but Brandenburg claims that there was probably a porticoed forecourt in front of the church entrance. He states that this atrium 'served to integrate the large architectural body of the basilica into the urban structure, and in particular to create a monumental access to the southern road leading to and named after the *porta Asinaria*'.[15] It is likely that the doors led to the central nave, direct access to the side aisles from the outside being impossible, as is customary in most palaeo-Christian basilicas in Rome. The Lateran's monumental size conveyed one central notion: the authority of the newly recognised faith, Christianity, and its earthly exponent, the Bishop of Rome.

The nineteen columns in the nave were made of red granite, those towards the side aisles, twenty-one to be exact, of green marble. Both red and green columns were *spolia*, that is recycled material from other buildings.[16] According to the *Liber Pontificalis*, it would be an understatement to say that Constantine was generous in equipping the new building with furnishings. This was a fine contrast with its exterior, which was kept plain and austere. Such a simple exterior, comparable to the Konstantinbasilika in Trier, was rather common in secular and functional Roman buildings, such as baths, or even the Basilica Nova of Maxentius in the Forum Romanum, yet the sacred architecture of the period was very different, with its conventional adornments of columns, cornices, entablatures, ashlar and stucco veneers.

The interior was of a splendour rarely seen. Not only were there marble columns, the walls were also covered with marble slabs. It is, however, impossible to have a precise idea of the marble decorations as the remains are insufficient as a basis for a serious analysis. Yet from contemporary buildings in which we can still see remains of the *opus sectile* (an art form similar to mosaics), we know that thin slabs of marble or other stone were laid in fields, frames and colourful patterns.

The roof and the half-dome of the apse are, in a Christian setting, of particular importance, and Constantine made sure that here too decoration was on a par with the grandeur of the architectural *ensemble*. In the half-dome of the apse, where the bishop's throne stood, there was a golden mosaic (although the figures on it only appeared later on). With these decorative elements in mind, it should come as no surprise that the church was called *aurea* – 'the golden one'.

With regards to the wealth of furnishings, it is interesting to note that seven altars were provided for, each with a large, free-standing silver candelabrum, yet it is unlikely that all seven were sacrificial altars; they were rather used to receive donations or for other ceremonial offerings and practices. The main altar stood in the western part of the nave, where it stands to this very day, right behind the triumphal arch. The basilica was also equipped with 169 silver chandeliers with numerous lamps to provide light.

The Lateran baptistery was probably built at the same time as the basilica, and at close proximity. It is a circular edifice with a diameter of 20m, in the centre of which was a circle of 8.50m destined to accommodate the baptismal font. Eight columns made of porphyry, from the imperial quarries in Egypt, gave the baptistery both an imperial and theological meaning, for in this context the number eight symbolises the resurrection of Christ on the eighth day.

This is one of only two liturgical basilicas inside the walls of the city, the other being Helena's basilica, known as the Basilica in Palatio Sessoriano in the *Liber Pontificalis*, but later named Santa Croce in Gerusalemme. The other six Constantinian churches are *martyria* outside the walls of the city.

The most famous of those is Saint Peter's, built on a former pagan and Christian necropolis, and currently the site of the Vatican. The basilica was built in honour of Saint Peter about a decade after the Lateran. The construction process was particularly challenging due to the slope of the hill. Old St Peter's Basilica, as we call it today, consisted of a wide central nave and two smaller aisles to each side, which were each divided by twenty-two marble columns sourced from *spolia*. Once again, this was a building of a magnificent size, in fact the largest of all of Constantine's churches: more than 350ft long, and 100ft tall.

Constantinople and Jerusalem

Constantine had great ambitions to equip Constantinople, his new capital of the Roman Empire, with churches of a particular splendour.

Construction of the original church of Hagia Sophia (Church of the Holy Wisdom) was started by Constantine as early as AD 325, on the site of a pagan temple. It was initially known as the Megale Ekklesia ('Great Church'). Following a fire in AD 404, the church was restored. The Nika riot in January AD 532, however, destroyed the church entirely, giving Justinian the opportunity to build a structure very similar to the one now standing. Constantine's church, which was not finished until the end of the reign of his son, Constantius II in 360, was a large edifice: it had an elongated central nave, four side aisles, a library and a baptistery of considerable size.

Just next to the Hagia Sophia, Constantine built the Hagia Eirene (Basilica of Holy Peace). The current structure dates back to the sixth century, and is particularly interesting for its *synthronon* in the apse, five rows of theatre-style stone seats for use by members of the clergy. The only decoration currently visible, a golden mosaic with a black cross, is a fine example of eighth-century iconoclasm.

The Church of the Holy Apostles merits a special mention, as it is Constantine's own *martyrium*, but we have very limited information on the original structure.

Constantine and his court also built churches in the Holy Land. The Holy Sepulchre stands on a site that is believed to encompass both Golgotha, or Calvary, where Jesus was crucified, and the tomb (sepulchre) where he was buried. It consists of a covered basilica, the stone of Golgotha and the tomb of Christ. In AD 335 the church was formally dedicated with an oration by Constantine's biographer, Eusebius of Caesarea. The Church of the Nativity in Bethlehem centred around three major architectural sections: an octagonal rotunda, a boxed atrium area of 45m by 28m and a double-aisled forecourt 29m by 28m.

8

Constantinian Art

Introduction

The most interesting aspect of the development of Roman art under Constantine's reign is the flourishing of Christian art with the financial support of the state. Under Constantine's patronage, churches were erected and richly decorated to give an image of authority and power. It is therefore recommended to look at mosaics and sarcophagi, but before that, let us first analyse the ultimate symbol of power and authority a Roman emperor could display: an arch of triumph.

An eclectic triumphal arch in Rome

It is from the Etruscans that the Romans learnt how to construct arches. This triggered a revolution in Roman architecture, as arches were used in the construction of bridges, aqueducts, amphitheatres and domed temples. When Constantine entered Rome after his victory against

Maxentius at the Milvian Bridge in October AD 312, the notion of a triumphal arch was not new, rather it was the continuation of a tradition started centuries earlier.

To this very day, the arch stands proudly between the Colosseum and the Palatine Hill. It was ordered by the Roman Senate to celebrate Constantine's victory, as was the tradition. The arch is remarkable for both its size and elegance, and especially its eclectic mix of *spolia* dating back to three distinct periods, namely the Imperial reliefs of Trajan, Hadrian and Marcus Aurelius. From an art historical perspective, the arch is situated at the crossroads of Classical and Late Antiquity, but not, as sometimes thought, of paganism and Christianity. Only in the arch's inscription *instinctu divinitatis* (inspired by the divine) or the image of Sol Invictus could one, with some creative thinking, recognise a modest reference to Christianity, albeit a quite unlikely one. The arch can be seen as separating the city from the outside; a triple distinction can be made to analyse the structure – east-west, north-south, above-below.

The horizontal frieze is best studied while walking around the monument, starting from the western side and going counter-clockwise. On the western frieze, one sees the *profectio*: Constantine leaving Milan with his soldiers, going towards the outside world for a military campaign. On the southern side, on the left one, is depicted the *obsidio*: there stands a tree, symbol of the countryside, and the Siege of Verona; on the southern frieze we see the *proelium*: the Battle of Milvian Bridge. Continuing to the east side, one sees the *ingressus*: the entry of Constantine with his army into Rome. Finally, on the northern frieze are portrayed the *oratio*, Constantine speaking to the citizens on the Forum Romanum, and the *liberalitas* with Constantine distributing money to the people.

Above the frieze, there are pairs of round reliefs over each lateral archway, dating to the rule of Emperor Hadrian, and framed in porphyry. They reflect various hunting scenes: on the north side, a boar hunt, a sacrifice to Apollo, a lion hunt and a sacrifice to Hercules. The southern side's round reliefs depict the departure for the hunt, a sacrifice to Silvanus, a bear hunt and a sacrifice to Diana. On these reliefs the heads of Hadrian have been transformed into the heads of Constantine, Constantius Chlorus and Licinius. The lateral sides (east and west) show medallions dating to Constantine's time: Sol Invictus is depicted on the east side (this, for Christians, could very possibly have been seen as 'he who brings the light'). The west medallion displays the moon.

On the south side, four panels depicting war scenes originate from a monument honouring Marcus Aurelius. On the north, the panels show the emperor leaving the city (probably Milan, but possibly Trier or Turin)[17] and arriving in Rome, as well as the *largitio*, the emperor distributing gifts to the people, and *clementia*, the emperor speaking to a conquered enemy.

Four panels from Trajan's Dacian Wars show violent scenes and, similarly to the decorations inherited from Hadrian and Marcus Aurelius, Trajan's military success is projected onto Emperor Constantine. Eight Dacian captives wearing Phrygian hats can be seen on the cornice above the columns.

The Arch of Constantine was the inspiration for many modern arches and buildings, such as the Arc de Triomphe and Arc de Triomphe du Carrousel in Paris, the Brandenburg Gate in Potsdam, Marble Arch in London, Kedleston Hall in Derbyshire, the Siegestor in Munich and the American Museum of Natural History in New York City. Yet the finest example without a doubt is Union Station in Washington DC, which integrates classical inspiration from both the Arch of Constantine in the main façade and the baths of Diocletian in its great vaulted spaces.

The fourth-century mosaics

of Santa Costanza

On the Via Nomentina in north-east Rome stands a fourth-century church named Santa Costanza. The building has particularly well-preserved mosaics which finely illustrate the developing Christian art in the early days of the faith's newly found glory. Santa Costanza is constructed in a circular form, with an ambulatory surrounding a central dome. It was built adjacent to the cemeterial Basilica of Saint Agnes, which is now in ruins, and constructed over catacombs. The building is a mausoleum, and is traditionally thought to have been built under the reign of Constantine for his daughter Constantina. Recent research has added nuance to this understanding and it may be the case that the mausoleum was built for Helena, another of Constantine's daughters.

The mosaic which decorated the central dome is missing, but both of the mosaics in the apses, and the mosaics in the ambulatory, remain and are to be seen as significant examples of early Christian art. The dating of the mosaics is not certain, but they are probably contemporary with the rest of the decoration, that is, fourth century.

The earliest surviving examples of mosaics representing Christ as the Pantocrator ('Ruler of All') can be seen in these two apses. The mosaic in the apse situated in the northern part of the ambulatory shows the beardless (but originally bearded) Pantocrator, his right hand lifted up high and an opened scroll of the law in his left, which he gives to St Peter. It is traditionally said that the image portrays a scene known as *Dominus legem dat* ('the Lord gives the law'), but that is not the case, as one can clearly read *Dominus pacem dat* ('the Lord gives peace'). It may be that these notions, *Pacem dat* and *Legem dat*, were fairly interchangeable, and in a Christian spirit the Law might very well be connected to Peace, but synonyms they are not. One might, however, connect the two by referring to the Edict of Milan which, from a legal standpoint, brought peace to the Church. In any case, as in Judaism, the Law was brought by Moses; Christianity may perhaps be seen here in a similar framework, in which Christ brings the Law. *Pacem* may very well be an incorrect restauration of *Legem* – for the time being, the mystery remains. The Pantocrator stands between palm trees and architectural structures representing the cities of Jerusalem and Bethlehem. To illustrate his authority over both heaven and earth, he is shown standing above the mountain of Paradise. Behind him one sees a relatively white sky with softly coloured clouds rising between Peter and Paul. The four evangelists are portrayed as sheep approaching Christ from two sides. This *traditio legis* ('handing over of the law') would remain one of the central themes of early Christian Art.

In the other mosaic, one sees a Pantocrator of a different nature, dressed in a darker robe and with a full beard. Here he is portrayed as ruler of the world, quite similar to an emperor or king, yet he is *verus rex*, the true king, seated on the globe. From there, he symbolically hands keys to St Peter.

The mosaics of the ambulatory are of a very different, but certainly no less interesting, nature. These decorations are essentially secular (and even Dionysiac) in nature. The seemingly stark contrast between the two types of mosaic is tempered by the fact that Christian art gradually integrated secular imagery, especially themes dealing with nature, agriculture and animal life. The combination of secular or pagan imagery with Christian scenes is also typical of the ambiguity of Constantine's reign. The panels in the ambulatory consist mainly of colourful geometrical patterns and elegant images of grapes, birds, fruit, harvesting and wine-making putti, and mythological figures. Two portrait busts are present in these mosaics, but their identification is uncertain; they may very well be Constantina and her husband.

Richly decorated Christian sarcophagi

In the Vatican museums, one finds a porphyry sarcophagus meant, most likely, for Constantina, which was originally in the Santa Costanza mausoleum. It was transported to the Vatican museums in 1790 on a cart dragged by forty oxen. The coffin is richly decorated on all four sides, with Dionysian imagery depicting garlands, grape vines and wine-making putti (similar to the mosaics in the ambulatory in Santa Costanza). Another larger and quite monumental sarcophagus currently stands in the same room of the Vatican museum, the Greek Cross Hall of the Pio Clementino Museum. This sarcophagus is believed to have held the remains of Helena, mother of Constantine. It was brought to the Vatican in 1777 from the imperial mausoleum at Tor Pignattara. In contrast with the decoration on Constantina's sarcophagus, here one sees military scenes and lions, Roman soldiers on horseback and barbarians, which leads some scholars to believe that the coffin was meant for a male family member in the first instance.

By the middle of the fourth century, under imperial patronage Christianity had become a part of the establishment. Many members of the elite of Roman society were new converts. Junus Bassius, a member of a senatorial family, was such an individual. His sarcophagus, which can be dated to AD 359, reflects the iconography and style of early Christianity's changed status in Roman society. It presents two horizontal registers of decorations, each containing five religious scenes from both the Old and New Testaments. In the centre of the upper layer one sees the *traditio legis*, Christ giving the law, a formula in Roman art to illustrate Christ as the sole source of law, as in the mosaics. Standing beside a youthful and beardless Christ seated on a throne are Saints Peter and Paul. On the left of the *traditio legis* are the Sacrifice of Isaac and the Arrest of Peter. To the right, a double scene of the Trial of Jesus before Pontius Pilate. In the centre of the lower layer is Christ's entry into Jerusalem (the *adventus*, typical of imperial art), and on the left are two niches representing Job on the dunghill and Adam and Eve. To the right of Christ's entry into Jerusalem are depicted Daniel in the lion's den and the Arrest of Paul.

Constantine's triumphal arch, the mosaics of Santa Costanza and Junus Bassius's sarcophagus illustrate the fact that Christian art in the fourth century did not reject classical elements, rather the opposite: early Christian art incorporated the classical tradition and under Constantine's reign this blending of pagan, secular and Christian spheres was essential to the development of both Christian art and architecture.

9

Legacy

A reign spanning three decades

When analysing the life and actions of Rome's first Christian emperor, one is due to encounter major challenges. Many unknowns remain, such as his age at his death, looks, parts of his education and the true nature of his spiritual connection to paganism and Christianity. Perhaps it is best to evaluate Constantine's reign and life as an ever-changing and evolving paradigm. His rule lasted more than three decades, and inevitably the Constantine of AD 337 was different from the young man appointed as one of the four tetrarchs of the Roman Empire by his father's troops in York in AD 306. The dynamic nature of the Roman emperor's personality, who was continuously progressing into Christianity throughout his life after AD 312, makes it a challenge, if not an impossible pursuit, to describe him from one perspective, or with merely one adjective. It would be unreasonable to neglect the polyparadigmatic nature of both Constantine's reign and character.

Still, historical evidence points to a few characteristics which remained a constant throughout his life: an unlimited ambition, both on the political and military level; strong diplomatic skills, which won him the simultaneous appreciation of both the pagan establishment and senatorial elites and the Christian communities he joined over the course of his life; and an exceptional military talent, which won him multiple successes in military campaigns throughout his leadership.

A new Rome in the East

In AD 324, Constantine announced a New Rome, strategically positioned on the banks of the Bosphorus, and renamed the existing city of Byzantium as Constantinople. This site was a wise option for both military and commercial reasons. From AD 324 until 330 major works were executed to make the city worthy of being the new capital of a great empire. Zosimus and an anonymous author describe the events of the official inauguration of the city on 11 May AD 330: a procession led to the forum and a statue of Apollo, its head replaced by another in Constantine's image, was placed on a porphyry column. Slowly but steadily the city would grow, both in population and politico-economic importance. Far from the ancient city of Rome, where Constantine had never spent much time, in Constantinople he could start with a blank sheet, designing the city's institutions, administration and architecture in accordance with his wishes.

The Donation of Constantine

The *Donatio Constantini* (Donation of Constantine) is a document probably produced in the eighth century, four centuries after the emperor's death in Nicomedia on 22 May AD 337. The text has Constantine refer to the Trinity, discuss his conversion to Christianity and his baptism, and declare a substantial donation to Pope Sylvester I (314–35). The *Donatio* records Constantine transferring to the pope the city of Rome and the western provinces of the empire, as well as ownership of the Lateran basilica and St Peter's, thereby elevating Sylvester to imperial dignity with all privileges and symbols pertaining to the imperial office. Furthermore, the document awarded 'supremacy as well over the four principal sees, Alexandria, Antioch, Jerusalem, and Constantinople, as also over all the churches of God in the whole earth'. The text was used to justify clerical authority in the various medieval struggles for power. However, in-depth research by the fifteenth-century Italian humanist Lorenzo Valla into the grammatical incoherence and unusual vocabulary used in the text showed the document to be a counterfeit.

Theocracy

Constantine accomplished what many had wished for during the imperial crisis of the Roman Empire in the third century: to reintroduce stable and continuous leadership, centralised power, persistent military triumphs, brilliant diplomacy, coupled with the exceptional ability – albeit it through Janus-faced strategies – to reunite the diverse communities and parts of the empire. The fact that he turned to Christianity, however one judges the sincerity of his conversion, seems to be the trigger for many of the crucial changes he brought to the Roman world. One may debate Constantine's family affairs, his economic, monetary and fiscal policies, or his surprising edicts and letters, of which around forty are still with us today. Yet it is through theological and legal initiatives that the emperor radically changed our world. His mixing of monotheism and state affairs; his injection of clergy in the secular legal structures via the *audientia episcopalis*; his bold support for Christianity, which would receive far more wealth and privileges than it had initially bargained for; and his subsequent architectural undertakings, which expressed his desire to give the Christians an unexpected level of authority, gladly accepted by the bishops, is what makes Emperor Constantine one of the most emblematic figures of Late Antiquity.

Did Constantine establish state Christianity? He certainly did not. Did Constantine willingly transfer secular political power to the Church? Apart from legal powers to settle disputes, which is a privilege not to be underestimated, he did not. Did Constantine create true religious liberty for all? A brief glance at the Edict of Milan might suggest so at first, but in reality he did not. What he did do, however, was create a politico-legal framework in which theocratic models could be established and grow. He laid the groundwork for medieval models of the competition between church and state. The equilibrium between those two spheres of power or, from another perspective, the absence of rivalry between religion and politics and/or law in Classical Antiquity, was from Constantine's reign onwards largely gone; now a single God and his army of bishops, presbyters and acolytes competed with another source of authority – the secular state. This created issues on the legal level, with various tensions arising because of differences in norms between secular and religious law. More importantly, to this very day it causes Western liberal democracies to reflect upon the nature of the state and its links and balance with religion. This conundrum knows political responses as varied as there are nations, and still causes challenges and problems that are not easily resolved.

It is the change in Christianity's status, namely from a persecuted sect on the fringes of Judaism, and marginalised within Roman society, to a political and judicial player, that is the true revolution of the fourth century. Often described as 'the Constantinian shift', some argue that it changed the very nature of Christianity. From this perspective, Emperor Constantine's decisions are seen as detrimental to Christian theology. The very fact that the clergy in fourth-century Rome gladly accepted its new status, escaping the terrible persecutions and assuming its new role, is still hard to accept for some Christian communities. Hence the initiatives advocating a return to what is generally seen as a pure form of Christian faith, far from the glitter and glamour that came with all the advantages and entitlements Constantine provided. Some Christian communities would go as far as refusing to celebrate mass in churches, claiming that house churches, as in a pre-Constantinian Christian context, are the best setting for religious gatherings. Although these remain minoritarian practices, they are a direct response to the developments which took place immediately after Constantine's conversion.

This leads us to what may be seen as Constantine's ultimate decision, for it may be the most impactful, namely his choice of the basilica, previously used as a commercial exchange and especially court of law, as the architectural expression of a legitimised Christianity. The basilica has remained the preferred choice for church construction since the fourth century, albeit with slight architectural diversity which is a natural result of the creative nature of the architectural profession and differing local building practices. But if one may generalise slightly when looking back at the influence of Constantine over the past seventeen centuries, Constantine's strength and legacy lie in his architectural course of action, which is not yet fully understood, but whose results are still with us nevertheless. It suffices to take a short walk in just about any city in Western Europe today to see a medieval or modern church whose architectural plans are largely based on the basilica form Constantine and his entourage selected after his victory at the Battle of the Milvian Bridge.

While the Roman Empire is long gone, many of its magnificent monuments in ruins and much of its multifaceted history still undiscovered or misinterpreted, it is through his unprecedented building programme, and his various avant-garde legal stipulations still with us today in one form or another, that Emperor Constantine maintains a presence among us, seventeen centuries after his glorious reign.

Notes

1   Jacob Burckhardt, *The Age of Constantine the Great*, pp. 292–306.
2   Edward Gibbon, *The History of the Decline and Fall of the Roman Empire, Vol. 2*, pp. 295–307.
3   Licinius is said to have had a similar vision during prayer, which was communicated by an angel and repeated by the whole army before they engaged Maximin's legions.
4   Henri Grégoire, 'La Conversion de Constantin', *Revue de l'Université de Bruxelles*, 36 (1930), pp. 231–72.
5   Louis Duchesne, *Histoire Ancienne de l'Eglise, Tome II*, p. 60.
6   The growing tensions between orthodoxy and heresy (for example, in the gnostic controversies and the writings of Irenaeus amongst others) were a clear sign of an attempt, at times successful, to create differences and set boundaries between 'us' and 'them', not least with the aim to fabricate frontiers between Jews and early Christians. These identity constructs were not watertight, however, and syncretism existed, and still exists, except in extremely isolated communities (even in the closed world of Hasidic dynasties one can hardly deny the various syncretic influences).
7   Lactantius, *De Mortibus Persecutorum*, 48.
8   *Codex Justinianus*, lib. 3, tit. 12, 3; translated by Philip Schaff in *History of the Christian Church, Vol. III* (New York: Charles Scribner, 1884), p. 380.

9 Derived from the Greek οἰκουμενικός, 'ecumenical' means 'worldwide' but is generally assumed to be limited to the Roman Empire in this context.

10 Eusebius of Caesarea counted 220, Athanasius of Alexandria counted 318 and Eustathius of Antioch counted 270 bishops.

11 See Everett Ferguson *Baptism in the Early Church: History, Theology, and Liturgy in the First Five Centuries*.

12 Jack Cottrell, *Baptism: A Biblical Study*, p. 7.

13 On the twenty canons, see P. Schaff and H. Wace, *A Select Library of Nice and Post-Nicene Fathers of the Christian Church*, pp. 2–42.

14 For more on Constantine and the *Vita sancti Silvestri*, see Wilhelm Pohlkamp, 'Kaiser Konstantin, der heidnische und der christliche Kult in den Actus Silvestri', *Frühmittelalterliche Studien*, Volume 18, May 2010, pp. 357–400.

15 H. Brandenburg, *Ancient churches of Rome from the fourth to the seventh century: the dawn of Christian architecture in the West*, p.23

16 See Joseph Alchermes, 'Spolia in Roman Cities of the Late Empire: Legislative Rationales and Architectural Reuse', *Dumbarton Oaks Papers*, Vol. 48 (1994), pp. 167–78.

17 Jack Carlson, 'Narrative Reliefs of the Arch of Constantine and the *Panegyrici Latini*', *New England Classical Journal* 37.3 (2010) 163–76.

Timeline

27 February 272–77	Birth of Flavius Valerius Constantinus in Naissus
293	Constantine's father, Constantius Chlorus, is appointed Caesar
293–94	Constantine becomes a military tribune
298	Military campaign against the Persians with Galerius
295–300	Marriage to Minervina and birth of Constantine's first son, Crispus
305	Constantius Chlorus becomes Augustus and Constantine joins his father in Gaul
25 July 306	Constantius Chlorus dies in Eboracum (York) and Constantine succeeds him
307	Marriage to Fausta, Maxentius's sister
28 October 312	Turns to Christianity and defeats Maxentius at the Battle of the Milvian Bridge in Rome
February 313	Edict of Milan officially ends persecutions of the Christians

Summer 313	Military campaign against the Alemanni
315	Decennalia and dedication of the Arch of Constantine in Rome
318	Establishment of the *audientia episcopalis*
321	Constantine proclaims the Sunday Rest Law
324	Constantine defeats Licinius at the Battle of Chrysopolis and becomes sole emperor
325	Vicennalia and First Council of Nicaea
329	Constantine's mother Helena dies
11 May 330	Consecration of Constantinople
335	Tricennalia
22 May 337	Death of Emperor Constantine in Nicomedia

Bibliography

Alchermes, Joseph, 'Spolia in Roman Cities of the Late
    Empire: Legislative Rationales and Architectural
    Reuse', *Dumbarton Oaks Papers*, Vol. 48 (1994),
    pp. 167–78.
Bardill, Jonathan, *Constantine, Divine Emperor of the
    Christian Golden Age* (Cambridge: Cambridge
    University Press, 2011).
Barnes, Timothy D., *Constantine and Eusebius*
    (Cambridge, MA: Harvard University Press, 1981).
Boin, Douglas, *Coming Out Christian in the Roman World*
    (London: Bloomsbury Press, 2015).
H. Brandenburg, *Ancient churches of Rome from the fourth
    to the seventh century: the dawn of Christian architecture
    in the West*, (Turnhout: Brepols, 2005)
Brent, Allen, *A Political History of Early Christianity*
    (London: T & T Clark, 2009).
Burckhardt, Jacob, *The Age of Constantine the Great* (New
    York: Pantheon, 1949).
Cottrell, Jack, *Baptism: A Biblical Study* (Joplin, MO:
    College Press Publishing Company, 1990).
Curran, John, *Pagan City and Christian Capital: Rome in
    the Fourth Century* (Oxford: Clarendon Press, 2000).
de Blaauw, Sible, *Cultus et Decor: Liturgia e architettura
    nella Roma Tardoantica e Medievale* (Vatican City:
    Biblioteca Apostolica Vaticana, 1994).

Dillon, John Noël, *The Justice of Constantine: Law, Communication, and Control* (Ann Arbor, MI, University of Michigan Press, 2012).

Doig, Allan, *Liturgy and Architecture: From the Early Church to the Middle Ages*, (Aldershot: Ashgate, 2008).

Dörries, Hermann, *Constantine and Religious Liberty* (New Haven, CT: Yale University Press, 1960).

Drake, H.A., *Constantine and the Bishops: The Politics of Intolerance* (Baltimore, MD: Johns Hopkins University Press, 2000).

Duchesne, Louis, *Histoire Ancienne de l'Eglise, Tome II* (Paris: Albert Fontemaing, 1907).

Dungan, David L., *Constantine's Bible: Politics and the Making of the New Testament* (Minneapolis, MN: Fortress, 2007).

Eadie, John William, *The Conversion of Constantine* (New York: Holt, Rinehart and Winston, 1971).

Eusebius, *Life of Constantine*.

Ferguson, Everett, *Baptism in the Early Church: History, Theology, and Liturgy in the First Five Centuries* (Grand Rapids, MI: Wm. B. Eerdmans Publishing Company, 2009).

Gibbon, Edward, *The History of the Decline and Fall of the Roman Empire, Vol. 2*, ed. J.B. Bury (London: Methuen & Co., 1896).

Grant, Michael, *Constantine the Great: The Man and his Times* (New York: Scribner's, 1994).

Grégoire, Henri, 'La Conversion de Constantin', *Revue de l'Université de Bruxelles*, 36 (1930), pp. 231–72.

Harries, Jill, *Law and Empire in Late Antiquity* (Cambridge: Cambridge University Press, 1999).

Holloway, R. Ross, *Constantine and Rome* (New Haven, CT: Yale University Press, 2004).

Jones, A.H.M., *Constantine and the Conversion of Europe* (London: English Universities Press, 1948).

Kilde, Jeanne Halgren, *Sacred Power, Sacred Space: An Introduction to Christian Architecture and Worship* (Oxford: Oxford University Press, 2008).

Krautheimer, Richard, *Early Christian and Byzantine Architecture* (Harmondsworth: Penguin, 1965).

Lactantius, *De Mortibus Persecutorum*, in *Firmiani Lactantii Opera II*, ed. O.F. Fritzsche, Biblioteca Patrum Ecclesiasticorum Latinorum Selecta XI (Leipzig: Tauchnitz, 1844).

Leithart, Peter, *Defending Constantine: The Twilight of an Empire and the Dawn of Christendom* (Downers Grove, IL: IVP Academic, 2010).

Lenski, Noel, *The Cambridge Companion to the Age of Constantine* (Cambridge: Cambridge University Press, 2006).

Lieu, Samuel, and Dominic Montserrat, *Constantine: History, Historiography, and Legend* (London: Routledge, 2002).

MacMullen, Ramsay, *Constantine* (New York: Dial Press, 1969).

Odahl, Charles Matson, *Constantine and the Christian Empire* (London: Routledge, 2004).

Pohlkamp, Wilhelm, 'Kaiser Konstantin, der heidnische und der christliche Kult in den Actus Silvestri', *Frühmittelalterliche Studien*, Vol. 18 (May 2010), pp. 357–400.

Pohlsander, Hans A., *The Emperor Constantine* (London: Routledge, 1996).

Roldanus, Johannes, *The Church in the Age of Constantine: The Theological Challenges* (London: Routledge, 2006).

Rousseau, Philip, *A Companion to Late Antiquity* (Chichester: Wiley-Blackwell, 2009).

Schaff, P. and H. Wace, *A Select Library of Nice and Post-Nicene Fathers of the Christian Church, second series, Volume XII: The Seven Ecumenical Councils* (Edinburgh: T&T Clark, 1899).

Stephenson, Paul, *Constantine: Roman Emperor, Christian Victor* (New York: Overlook Press, 2010).

Van Dam, Raymond, *The Roman Revolution of Constantine* (New York: Cambridge University Press, 2007).

Webb, Matilda, *The Churches and Catacombs of Early Christian Rome* (Brighton: Sussex Academic Press, 2001).

White, Lloyd Michael, *The Social Origins of Christian Architecture Volumes I and II* (Valley Forge, PA: Trinity Press, 1996–97).

pocket GIANTS

A series about people who changed the world – and why they matter.

Series Editor – Tony Morris

www.thehistorypress.co.uk